GARDEN FURNITURE

A Practical Handbook for Woodworkers

GEORGE BUCHANAN

WARD LOCK

For Douggie

ACKNOWLEDGEMENTS

I am very grateful to Roy Oliver of Wessex Resins, Neil Truckle of International Paints, Michael Dark of Texas Homecare D.I.Y. Stores, Ron Mason and his colleagues at Bosch Tools Ltd, and John Lawrence and Co. (Dover) Ltd for providing me with technical advice, materials, information and help in designing and making this garden furniture, and Mr Stapleton of Golden Valley Nurseries who planted the plants in the planters. I would also like to thank my friends who welcomed us into their gardens for the photographs: Betsy and Michael Vincent, Honor and Theo Gimbel, Jane and Nick Parsons and Jan Peters, who also encouraged me to use her Orchard Bench in this book. My thanks also to my dear friend Douglas Peters. I have used his workshop in one of the photographs, and it was there that we spent many enjoyable evenings working together at his bench.

I must also thank Keasley Welch who quietly and firmly introduced me to the delights of modern word processing, and Elizabeth for her practical help, encouragement and support.

DISCLAIMER

While every care has been taken over the accuracy of the information in this book, the author and publisher cannot be held responsible for any accidents related to products used by readers, or to their workmanship.

First published in 1991 by Ward Lock
Villiers House, 41/47 Strand, London WC2N 5JE

A Cassell imprint

© George Buchanan 1991

British Library Cataloguing in Publication Data
Buchanan, George, *1948–*
   Garden furniture.
   1. Gardens furniture design & construction
   I. Title
   684.18

ISBN 0–7063–6977–7

Typeset by Columns Design and Production Services Ltd, Reading
Printed and bound by The Bath Press

CONTENTS

LEVEL OF DIFFICULTY CHART

Project	Essential power tools drill jigsaw orbital sander router	Circular saw	Belt-sander	Planer	All-purpose saw PFL 550-PE	Lathe	Extra clamps	Mortice and tenon	Mitre joint	Cross-halving	Scarf	Groove and fillet	Angled mortice and tenon	Decorative back	Cost	Time	Rating
Garden seat	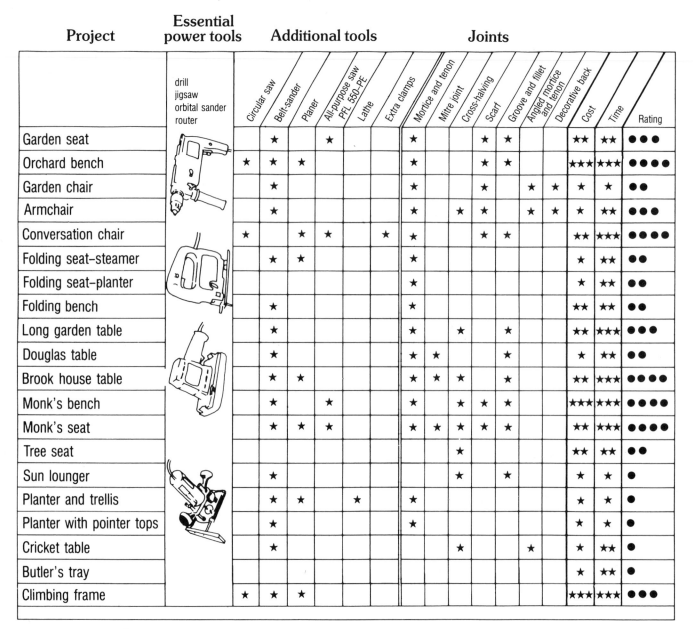		★		★		★				★	★			★★	★★	●●●
Orchard bench		★	★	★			★				★	★			★★★	★★★	●●●●
Garden chair			★				★				★		★	★	★	★	●●
Armchair			★				★			★	★		★	★	★	★★	●●●
Conversation chair		★		★	★		★				★	★			★★	★★★	●●●●
Folding seat–steamer			★	★			★								★	★★	●●
Folding seat–planter							★								★	★★	●●
Folding bench			★				★								★★	★★	●●
Long garden table			★				★			★		★			★★	★★★	●●●
Douglas table			★				★	★				★			★	★★	●●
Brook house table			★	★			★	★	★			★			★★	★★★	●●●●
Monk's bench			★		★		★		★	★	★				★★★	★★★	●●●●
Monk's seat			★	★	★		★	★	★	★	★				★★	★★★	●●●●
Tree seat									★						★★	★★	●●
Sun lounger			★						★		★				★	★	●
Planter and trellis			★	★	★		★								★	★	●
Planter with pointer tops			★				★								★	★	●
Cricket table			★							★			★		★	★★	●
Butler's tray															★	★★	●
Climbing frame		★	★	★											★★★	★★★	●●●

NOTE

The woodworking projects in this book have been designed to be built using basic woodworking hand tools, and Bosch hand-held and bench-mounted electric power tools have been used in this particular instance. Not every make of D.I.Y. power tools is capable of the work load and flexibility demanded here. For those thinking of equipping their workshop with additional tools, it may help them to know that these designs are based on the capabilities of the Bosch D.I.Y. tool range. If in doubt, contact your local supplier of D.I.Y. materials. A general note of suppliers is listed at the back of this book.

INTRODUCTION

THIS book gives you the opportunity to create your own classic wooden garden furniture, which will decorate and enhance your garden, and be a joy to use.

The furniture is built using straightforward traditional joints. No special experience or skill is required and, although some familiarity in handling the tools is assumed, for those new to woodworking there are special sections which feature some of the tricks and techniques used by woodworkers.

Each project is accompanied by dimensioned drawings and full illustrated instructions, which give both Imperial and metric dimensions. To avoid cluttering the drawings, standard planed woodsections are marked by a letter, and their size can be read from the table at the side of the drawings.

The furniture is made from solid wood, using generous sizes for strength and durability. In the designs, care has been taken to allow air to circulate between the timbers to minimise the number of damp and inaccessible spots where rot might develop. Pine or spruce is used throughout – they are not durable woods, but they are cheap and can be bought planed in standard sizes from D.I.Y. stores and timber merchants.

Other woods can be used instead. Teak and Brazilian mahogany are durable, strong and pleasant woods to work. Cedar of Lebanon is cheap and durable, but weak. Unless a wood is specified, cedar, pine, spruce, or teak is suitable for any of the designs in this book. The relatively substantial wood sizes, and the finishing schedules using microporous paints, stains and epoxy resin ensure the furniture will last.

In order to make any of these projects, you will need the basic woodworking tools described on pages 11–15, a bench and a suitable workshop. In addition to the hand tools it will be a great help to have a number of hand-held electric tools, including a router, a jigsaw, and a sander. If you plan to make the furniture from rough-sawn woods obtained from country wood-yards, you will also need a circular saw or bandsaw to mill the larger pieces of timber.

If you allow yourself the time and luxury of working carefully and well, you will be able to create some delightful and unique pieces of garden furniture.

CHOICE OF WOOD

Your choice of wood will depend on your budget, your ability to machine rough-sawn wood into suitable sizes, the finish you want to apply, and the amount of time you can set aside for the project.

If your prime considerations are cost and the need for wood ready-sawn and planed to standard sizes, you will have to buy pine or spruce. It is cheap, and readily available in the sizes specified in these designs from D.I.Y. stores and timber merchants. Unfortunately, pine and spruce cannot be left unfinished: they are non-durable woods and, unless properly finished, will not last more than four or five years without rotting. So the furniture will have to be protected from weathering with the full paint, stain or epoxy resin finishing schedules specified on page 120.

If you have the capacity to machine rough-sawn wood, cedar of Lebanon or larch will be equally cheap, and a much more durable alternative to pine or spruce. Unfinished furniture made from these woods will survive prolonged exposure, and with regular doses of wood preservative will last many years.

Wood	Durability	Recommended finish
Teak	Very durable	Unfinished or oiled
Iroko	Very durable	Oiled, or finished with microporous stain or paint. Unfinished Iroko weathers from a green/yellow to deep brown
Afrormosia	Very durable	Microporous stain or paint.
Luan	Moderately durable	Paint, microporous stain, clear epoxy resin finish.
Brazilian Mahogany	Durable	Epoxy sealer, followed by polyurethane two-part paint finish. Alternatively, follow epoxy with tinted U.V. inhibiting polyurethane varnish.
Oak	Durable	Leave unfinished.
Larch	Moderately durable	Can be left unfinished, occasionally coating with clear preserver. Paint, or microporous stain.
W. Red Cedar	Durable	Unfinished or microporous stain or paint.
Cedar of Lebanon	Durable	As larch.
Douglas Fir	Moderately durable	West clear epoxy finish, or microporous stain or paint.
Pine (deal) (Norway spruce, Scots and Baltic pine)	Non durable	Preservative, then microporous paint or stain. Epoxy finish (clear) followed by U.V. Varnish.
Sequoia	Durable	Leave unfinished or use microporous paint or stain.

Rough-sawn and seasoned larch and cedar can be bought from country wood-yards (see List of Suppliers).

If you want to leave the furniture unfinished, to weather down to a silver or mottled grey, you must buy teak or oak. They are expensive woods, but they are the best for garden furniture because they are attractive, immensely strong, and very durable. However, teak and oak are hard, so tools need frequent sharpening and sawing, planing and routing all take longer. In terms of both material cost and labour they are the most expensive woods.

Timber importers have many other tropical hardwoods available, some of which are durable, and cheaper than teak. Iroko and keruing are used for making garden furniture, but are unpleasant to handle and, unless your workshop has an efficient dust extraction system, should be avoided. Other hardwoods are listed in the chart. When machined, many tropical hardwoods release dangerous dust so wear a face mask when machining them.

Glueing	Notes
Epoxy resin. May be necessary to wash off oily residue with solvent before glueing.	This is the ideal wood from which to make garden furniture.
Epoxy resin if left unfinished, otherwise resorcinol resin.	A splintery, tough wood to use, hard on the tools. Produces a foul, irritating dust when machined. Take all sensible precautions to extract dust from the workshop when using this wood.
Resorcinol or epoxy resin glue.	
Resorcinol or epoxy resin.	A rich brown-coloured wood, darkens as it is exposed to the air. A cheap alternative to Brazilian mahogany.
Resorcinol or epoxy resin. Do not use two part urea-formaldehyde glues — the acid hardener discolours the mahogany.	A clean-grained, attractive wood, predictable in use and easy to work.
Epoxy resin.	A tough wood, very attractive yellow/brown colour when newly cut, weathers to grey.
Epoxy resin for clear finish, otherwise resorcinol resin glue.	A strong wood, often too knotty to work easily. Choose clean lengths, with straight grain. White sapwood prone to worm. Resinous cracks and knots should be sealed with knotting before painting.
Epoxy resin, or resorcinol resin.	A very light wood, easy to work, but easily bruised. Leave furniture out of doors for several weeks before painting to allow oils to wash out of the wood.
As larch.	An easy wood to use, knot-free planks often difficult to find, but knots are enormous, not easily missed, and not often less than 90 cm (3 feet) apart. Some wastage will be expected, negotiate a useful price reduction.
Epoxy, resorcinol if painted.	Very strong, straight-grained. Apply knotting to resinous parts before finishing. Tends to splinter, so make sure all sharp corners are sanded smooth before finishing.
Epoxy or resorcinol.	Not an exterior wood. Suitable outside only if finishing schedules are followed. Choose knot-free pieces for stressed parts, such as chair legs. Readily available and very cheap.
Epoxy or resorcinol.	A light, weak wood, very easily bruised. Suitable for tables, but not chairs or climbing frames. Oily, and difficult to stain. Wash with white spirit and leave to dry before staining or painting.

There is a skill in matching timber to a particular use that most wood-yard managers will be glad to share. If you are buying wood from a timber merchant, explain your project to them. A good manager will select and deliver what you need. If there is a large selection of identically cut boards of the same species to choose from, and assistance is not available, the following hints might help you to choose the best pieces:

■ Knots

Large knots, particularly those with a black ring round them, weaken a board and are vulnerable to rot. Knots are the remains of twigs and branches that have been cut off, and enveloped as the tree has grown. Sometimes they will appear almost circular, at other times they will be long and picturesque. These latter are the most weakening, and can easily halve the strength of the plank

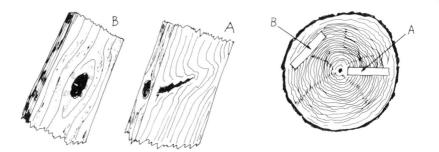

■ Warping

Do not buy wood that is twisted or bent, unless the wood is going to be cut into very short lengths and is cheap. Distorted wood will bend again after you have shaped it. The tensions locked inside the timber during growth which have already distorted the wood once, will bend the wood again, so upsetting your work, until the locked-in stresses reach a new equilibrium. This illustration shows the end section of a log, and some sample planks that have been cut from it. By comparing the pieces you buy with the illustrations in this book you will be able to gain an idea of the way in which the timber will warp and shrink in response to changes in humidity. With narrow planks, this should not be a major problem, but there are components in some of these designs, such as the Orchard Bench (see page 22) and the Planters (see page 100), where the wood is 125 mm (5 in) or more wide. These should be positioned with the heartwood uppermost.

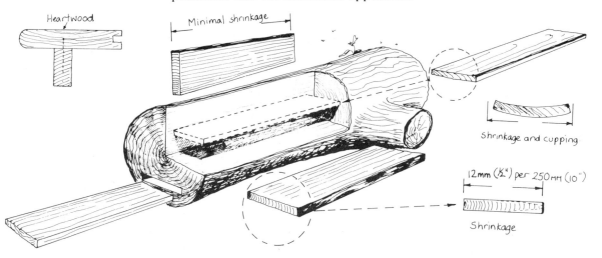

Heartwood

Minimal shrinkage

Shrinkage and cupping

12 mm (½") per 250 mm (10")

Shrinkage

■ Surface Roughness

If, despite being machine planed, the timber has a fine, fluffy, felt-like texture, avoid it. This is another sign of instability and is known as reaction or tension wood.

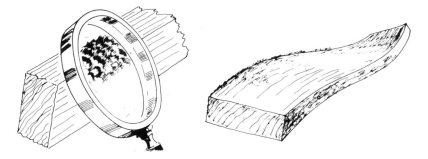

■ Black Streaks

Black streaks across the grain could indicate a fracture caused during felling; black streaks or patches on the surface are often a sign of rot. Superficial blemishes can usually be removed with a saturated solution of oxalic acid, which is obtainable from the suppliers listed in the back of the book.

■ Moisture Content

Most planks on sale in large timber or D.I.Y. stores will be sufficiently dry to use right away and it is only with timber that has been bought direct from a timber yard that you need to worry about the moisture content. The moisture content of the wood should be about 18%, which a wood-yard manager can measure for you using a moisture meter. If you are buying from a yard where wood has been stacked outside, allow approximately one year of drying for every 25 mm (1 in) of thickness. If the wood has been stacked so that undergrowth prevents air circulation, seasoning will take longer.

■ Grain

By looking at the grain, it is possible to predict how the wood will behave as it is cut and planed, and how it will split. The illustrations show comparative strengths of similar shaped pieces, with the grain running in different directions. Woods used with short grain are much weaker than those with the grain running lengthwise. Make sure that you arrange the wood correctly, as shown in the illustrations, for maximum strength, avoiding very short grain.

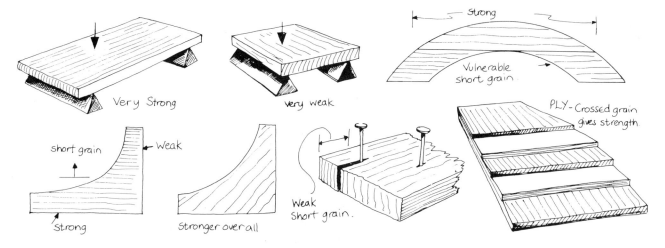

WOODWORKING – TECHNIQUES AND EQUIPMENT

Woodworking should be enjoyable. There are episodes in every job that are repetitive and physically demanding, and it is just as important to learn to find the pleasure in these, as it is to relish the final assembly, painting, public acclamation and approval. It is essentially a solitary hobby and one that creates a lot of mess so, to begin with, dedicate a space that can be put aside for woodworking, where others will not mind, or at least will tolerate, the noise and mess you make. You do not need much space, just room for a small bench or workmate, tools, and a place for your project. Have your machine tools and the hand tools in regular use on display and close at hand. Store others in a dry box or cupboard. Stick pictures on the wall for diversion and arrange plenty of lighting – a pair of fluorescent tubes and some halogen spotlights will be well worth installing. Keep the floor and the bench clean. Dispose of woodshavings and sawdust outside the workshop area as they are a fire hazard.

Woodworking is a much more delicate skill than many people believe and it is difficult to estimate how long the work will take. Try not to schedule your project, especially if you are only working on it part time. Know the order in which you are going to set about your project, and think ahead to the day's work before you get into the workshop. Time pressure should not make you work harder or faster than is enjoyable, practical or safe. Stop working before you come to a glueing-up job, unless you know you have all the time and more to see it through (glueing is covered in more detail on page 62). Use sharp tools as they are safer, require much less effort to handle, and do the job more quickly. Strop your edge tools regularly, and sharpen them as soon as they stop singing through the wood and start to chew it instead. Instructions for sharpening are on page 20.

Marking Out

Use sharp 'B' pencils, and a keen marking knife. Measure twice before marking and again, with reference to the work already completed. Measure once more before cutting.

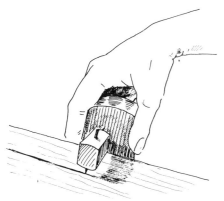

■ Marking Gauges

These gauges are useful for scoring lines parallel to an edge. They are held as shown. Minor adjustments are made by tapping the stick on the bench until the fence moves. It will be easy to use the gauge if the wood grain is parallel to the side of the timber. Where the grain diverges, press the fence up hard against the edge and, if necessary, reverse the direction of the gauge, so that the grain pulls its point into the timber.

■ Set Squares

These are used for marking right angles. They are braced against a planed or sawn edge, which should be identified with the mark illustrated.

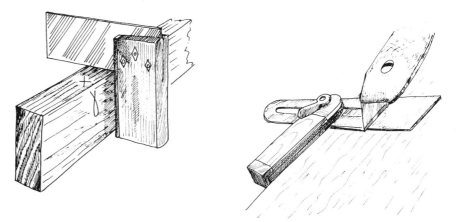

■ Sliding Bevel

The angle of the blade of the sliding bevel can be altered, and is locked by the fastening screw. It is used like a set square for marking off or transferring any angles.

■ Dumbstick or Dividers

Where a piece of timber has to be shaped to fit against an irregular structure, the irregular shape is transferred using a dumbstick or a pair of dividers locked to the appropriate setting. The illustrations show how this is done. It is important to remember that the offsets must be parallel, otherwise marking out will be inaccurate.

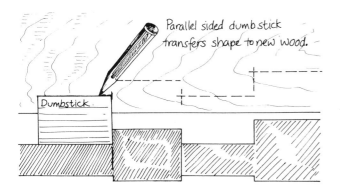

Parallel sided dumbstick transfers shape to new wood.

Dumbstick.

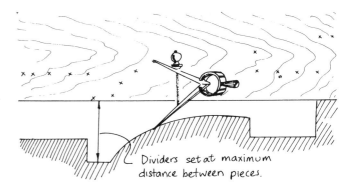

Dividers set at maximum distance between pieces.

Sawing

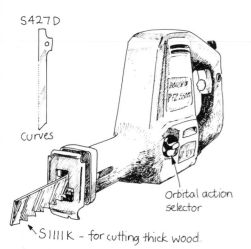

S427D

curves

Orbital action
selector

SIIIIK - for cutting thick wood.

■ All-purpose Saw

The orbital action of this saw enables thick stock to be cut quickly and quite accurately. Wood up to 150 mm (6 in) can be sawn, although with the thicker wood, care must be taken to ensure that the tip of the blade does not wander too far from the cutting line. Choose the right saw blade, tack a batten to the piece of wood you are cutting, tilt the saw back, and let the saw eat its way along the line. Use the minimum necessary horizontal pressure to achieve accurate results, and arrange a vacuum cleaner to remove the sawdust from the saw line. With a multi-purpose saw, which can be fitted with blades for straight cuts, curves, rasps and files, much of the effort of sawing, rounding and smoothing will be eliminated. For accurate work, it will be worthwhile filing a guide line to the saw bed to help line up the saw.

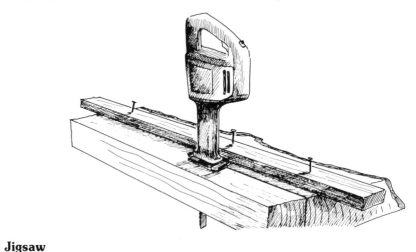

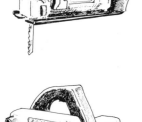

■ Jigsaw

This is a piercing saw, with a very narrow blade, capable of cutting very tight curves in thick wood (up to 65 mm/2½ in) accurately. If you do not have a jigsaw and are thinking of buying one, choose one with an orbital cutting action as they are much easier to use.

■ Circular Saw

This is an invaluable saw for cutting straight, parallel lines. Mounted under a saw bench, or equipped with a cutting fence, this saw will cut straight stock to size accurately and quickly. Wear safety glasses and ear mufflers when using a circular saw, and if you have it permanently mounted under a saw bench, use push sticks to press the wood into the blade. When using the circular saw as a hand tool, ensure that the wood you are cutting is properly supported and clamped.

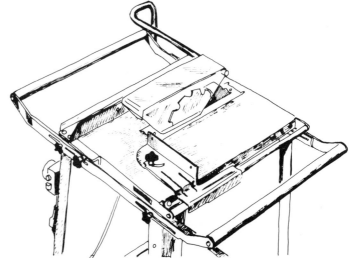

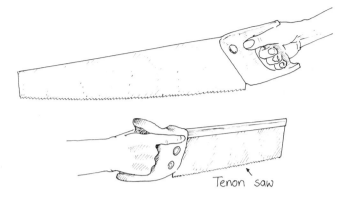
Tenon saw

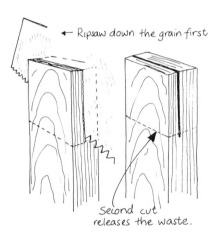
← Ripsaw down the grain first

Second cut releases the waste.

■ Handsaws

You will need two saws, a handsaw for rough and quick cutting, and a tenon saw for fine straight cuts. They are held as illustrated. Saws must be used lightly. If you apply heavy pressure to speed them up, they will wander off course. Start a cut at 45° to the surfaces of the wood. Raise the saw handle as the cut deepens. When sawing off a tenon cheek, for example, cut down the grain first, and snip off the cheek with a tenon saw afterwards. It weakens the wood less to over-run on the ripsaw cut down the grain, than to over-run on the cross grain sawcut.

To make a precise sawcut, incise the marking line with a very sharp hobby knife or scalpel, and then carve away the wood on the waste side of the line with a sharp chisel held at a slant. Lodge the tenon saw in the slight recess and, keeping it hard up against the edge, begin cutting. Make a bench hook to help hold your work.

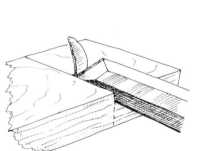

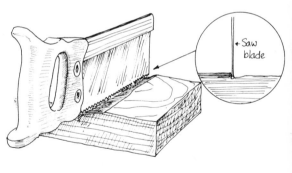
Saw blade

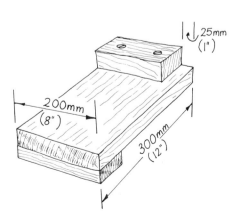
200mm (8")
300mm (12")
25mm (1")

Planing and Smoothing Wood

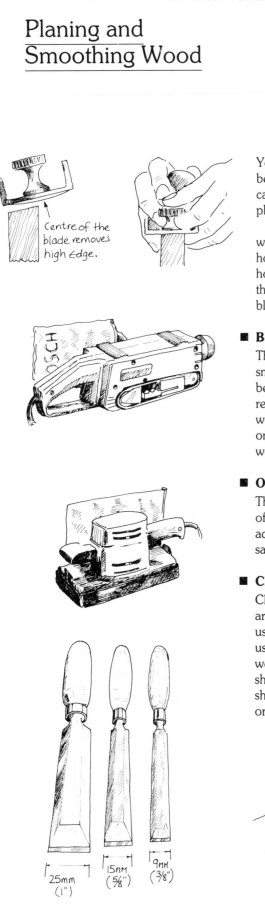

Centre of the blade removes high Edge.

You will need two planes, a smoothing plane and a block plane. They should be extremely sharp and finely adjusted, and cut with a clear crackle. Rub candle wax on the sole of the plane to make it easier to push. Use the block plane for delicate work, planing mitres and end grain.

Although planes will be bought new with a cutting edge exactly parallel with the sole, after a few sharpenings the edge becomes curved and cuts a hollow. Bear this in mind when trying to plane a piece of wood square. The hollow can be put to good use – high spots can be worked down by moving the plane sideways with the tips of your fingers, positioning the centre of the blade over the high spots.

■ Belt Sander

This is an invaluable power tool as it enables completed woodwork to be smoothed quickly. Hold the sander firmly with both hands as the edge of the belt will score your work if the sander is allowed to take control. Wood is removed more quickly if the sander is held at an angle to the grain of the wood. Some belt sanders can be fitted with clamps so that it can be mounted on the bench and used for delicate shaping. Always wear a face mask when working with a belt sander.

■ Orbital Sander

These are predictable, gentle tools that take all the toil out of the final stages of sanding the furniture. The square-cornered sanding pad allows sanding access to the most difficult corners. Wear a face mask when using an orbital sander as it produces extremely fine dust, which should not be inhaled.

■ Chisels

Chisels are dangerous. Handle them slowly and carefully. The sharper they are, the easier they are to use, so strop them every five or six cuts. They are usually held as illustrated, although for champhering and morticing they are used round the other way. Try not to press chisels too hard. Instead, use your weight and balance to apply the force, lodging your arms against your chest, shoulder or side, so they do not get tired. The three bevel-edged chisels shown are fragile and should be handled carefully, especially when morticing or trimming a mortice.

25mm (1")

15mm (5/8")

9mm (3/8")

Additional Equipment

■ Router

A router is an excellent tool for running grooves and rebates, plunging out mortices, and for mass producing components. A plunge router is necessary for making the projects in this book. For information on routing, see p. 82.

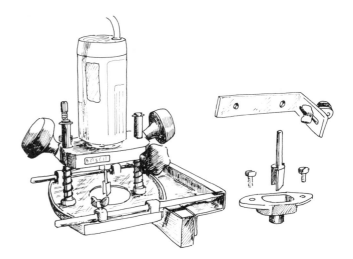

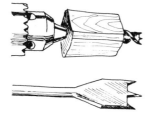

■ Drills

An electric drill, and five spade or brad-point drill bits (6 mm, 9 mm, 12 mm, 18 mm, 25 mm/¼ in, ⅜ in, ½ in, ¾ in, 1 in) will be required. If your drill is not fitted with an adjustable depth stop, make up some blocks from wood offcuts, drill through them, and have them at hand when you want to control the depth of the drill. Brad-point and spade bits have a centre point, and spurs at their circumference. They cut accurately and cleanly, and do not tear up the wood at the perimeter of the hole.

■ Hammers and Screwdrivers

An assortment of hammers and screwdrivers is needed.

■ Fastenings

For information on fastenings, see page 90.

GARDEN SEAT

THIS garden bench seats three people. Although it is simple to make, there are alternative designs for the back. Some of these are quite tricky but they give distinction to what is essentially a commonplace design. The back legs are swept back for stability. They are cut from straight stock, the waste from cutting the curved front of the leg, being glued to the back. The main framework is morticed and tenoned together. All the main rails are the same size and width except the front rail which is narrower. The seat is made from horizontal slats, set into grooves in the end frames with filler pieces between them. The seat slats are installed after the first end is glued and pegged. The armrests are cut from rectangular stock and are joined to the back legs with a lap, and a mortice and tenon joint. At the front, the armrests fit over stub tenons cut in the top of the front legs. The back can be fitted with vertical slats which slip into mortices in the top and lower frame. If you are going to fit a decorative geometrical back, tenon just one vertical slat in the centre of the back, the same thickness as the back rails. The geometric inserts are built up inside a cross-halved lightly constructed frame, which is trimmed after fabrication, slipped into the space between the rails and glued there.

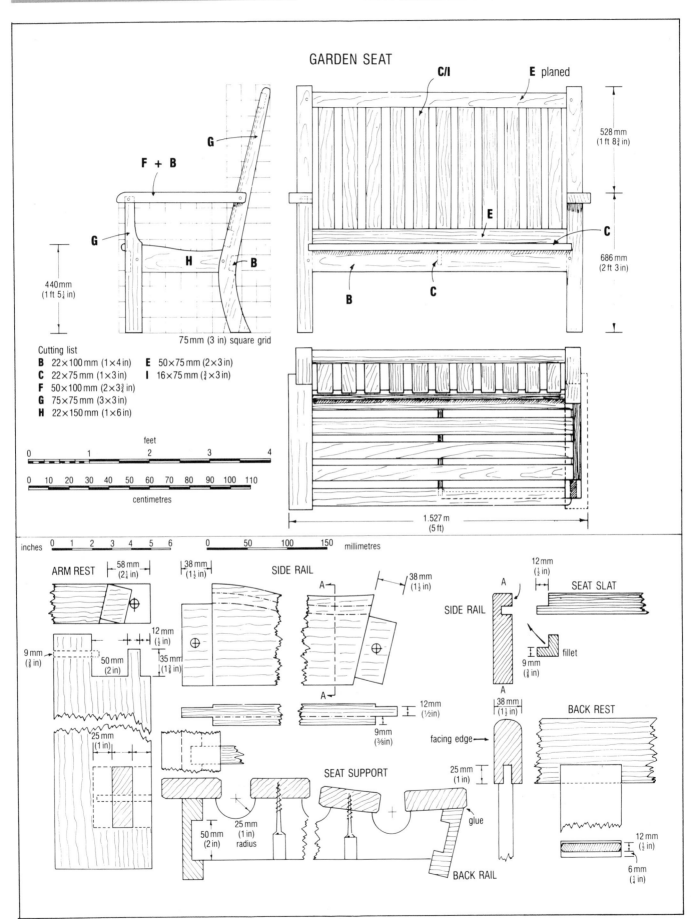

GARDEN SEAT

C/I   E planed

528 mm
(1 ft 8¾ in)

E

C

686 mm
(2 ft 3 in)

G

F + B

G

H   B

440mm
(1 ft 5¼ in)

B   C

75mm (3 in) square grid

Cutting list
B 22×100 mm (1×4 in)   E 50×75 mm (2×3 in)
C 22×75 mm (1×3 in)   I 16×75 mm (¾×3 in)
F 50×100 mm (2×3¾ in)
G 75×75 mm (3×3 in)
H 22×150 mm (1×6 in)

feet
0   1   2   3   4

0 10 20 30 40 50 60 70 80 90 100 110

centimetres

1.527 m
(5 ft)

inches 0 1 2 3 4 5 6   0   50   100   150   millimetres

ARM REST   58 mm
(2¼ in)

38 mm
(1½ in)

SIDE RAIL

38 mm
(1½ in)

A

A

12 mm
(½ in)

SEAT SLAT

SIDE RAIL

12mm
(½ in)

9 mm
(⅜ in)

50 mm
(2 in)

35 mm
(1⅜ in)

fillet

9 mm
(⅜ in)

A

A

12mm
(½in)

9mm
(⅜in)

25 mm
(1 in)

facing edge →

38 mm
(1½ in)

BACK REST

SEAT SUPPORT

25 mm
(1 in)

50 mm
(2 in)

25 mm
(1 in)
radius

glue

BACK RAIL

12 mm
(½ in)

6 mm
(¼ in)

Construction

Draw a full-sized end elevation of the bench on a large sheet of board. Make up the curved back legs, (see page 44) and when the glued joins are cured, clean them. Cut the front legs to length, remembering to include the stub tenons. Cut the side rails and armrests, and then the four main back and seat rails.

Front legs.

Shoulder line

reference line

■ Legs

Taking the back legs first, mark off the cut-off line for the bottom of the legs, making sure that the leg is leaning back at the correct angle. Using the full-sized end elevation drawing, mark up from the bottom of each leg the lower end of the seat mortices. This is a common measurement for all the legs, and should be used as a reference line from which other measurements can be taken, see page 17. Mark in the position of all the other mortices and the shoulders for the stub tenons, lifting the measurements directly from the drawing. Clamp the legs in pairs to transfer the marks to the second leg. Note that the mortice for the front rail is shallower, as the seat slat sits across it. Rout out all the mortices, using a two-flute 8 mm (3/8 in) cutter, holding the legs in the vice or router box. Apart from the armrest mortices, the fence setting can remain constant for all the mortices in the main framework.

Mark off and cut the stub tenons at the top of the front legs, see page 30.

■ Side Rails

Take the pieces for the side rails and, using the squared drawing on the plans, transfer the seat curve to the template. Mark the right-angled shoulders for the front legs, and the angled shoulder where the side rail meets the back legs. Take this angle from the full-scale drawing of the side elevation. Cut the side rail tenons and fit them into the legs. Drill them for pegging, and then rout the seat slat groove at the inside top of each rail.

■ Assembly of Frames

Peg up the side rails and legs, and fit the armrests. Mark the joint with the back legs by holding the armrest in position and pencilling off where the tenon and lap have to be cut. Then square off the joint, marking the angled shoulders from the drawing of the end elevation.

Saw down the sides of the tenon and the lap, and saw out the waste between the lap and the tongue with a jigsaw. Finish with a chisel and mallet, working from both sides of the armrest. When the back leg joint is completed, press the armrest in place, and mark off the position of the front stub tenon. Drill out the centre of the mortice, and then square it up with a chisel, until it fits. Now that the end frames are completed, they can be glued and pegged up. Pull the armrest tight into position with two tourniquets, one to the back leg, the other between the side rail and the armest, pulling the armrest down over the stub tenon.

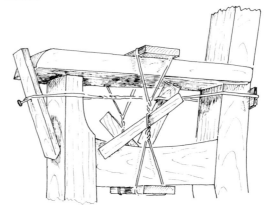

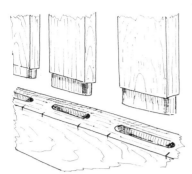

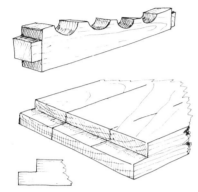

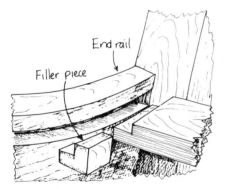

■ Back and Seat Rails

Cut and fit the tenons for the back and seat rails. The rails are all the same length and their shoulders are all at right-angles. Pair up the two back rails for marking out the slats if the seat is going to have a slatted back as shown in the plans, or the central reinforcement piece if it is going to be fitted with a decorative back. Rout out the mortices for the back, and then cut the slats to fit them, rounding their edges so that they slide easily into the routed mortices. Make up and assemble the back and glue it together, tensioning it with two or three lightly pulled up tourniquets, and holding it temporarily in position with the back legs of the two end frameworks.

■ Seat

Copying the curve from the end frame, cut out the curved seat support to fit between the front and back seat rails scalloping its top edge to allow moisture to drain from the joints with the seat slats. Mortice the support into the centre of the back and front rails. Glue up one end of the chair and peg both ends, so that one can be loosened to allow the seat slats to be slipped into position. When the glue has hardened, fit the seat slats.

Cut two suitably wide planks, so that all the slats can be sawn from just two pieces of wood, and cut them to length, remembering to add 25 mm (1 in) for the 12 mm (½ in) rebates at each end. Rout out the end rebates. Cut the planks down to 75 mm (3 in) widths using the circular saw.

Make up a short length of filling piece. Now, glue the end joints and fit the seat slats into place, alternating with a filler piece tapped into the groove. Use plenty of glue. Use a stainless steel panel pin to hold any loose filler pieces. For advice on making up the filler pieces, and other routing operations, see page 82.

Lastly, fit the front seat slat, glueing and screwing it onto the front rail. Fasten it from underneath, and slip a glue block into each front corner to support it.

Smooth the seat and remove the corners from the armrests, etc. with a belt sander fitted with a fine abrasive belt. Finish with an orbital sander. When this work is complete, fit the prefabricated decorative backs and paint the chair with microporous paint.

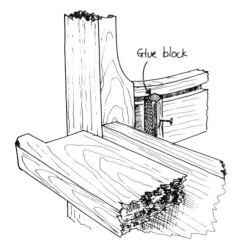

End rail

Filler piece

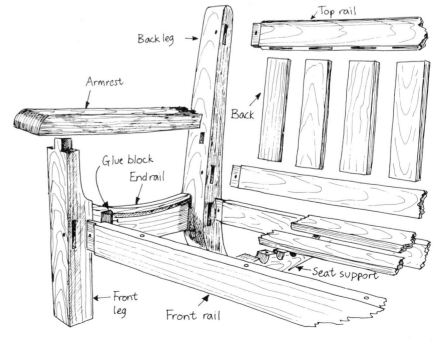

Glue block

Back leg

Armrest

Top rail

Back

Glue block

End rail

Seat support

Front leg

Front rail

SHARPENING TOOLS

Always use sharp tools. It requires less effort to cut with a sharp tool, and it is safer. You can tell if an edge tool is blunt by the way it performs. A sharp plane makes a high pitched crackle as it slices off the shavings. A blunt chisel cuts jerkily and leaves score marks. If a blade is sharp it ought to be possible to pare off a strip of paper. If it tears, stop work and sharpen the blade.

Chisels

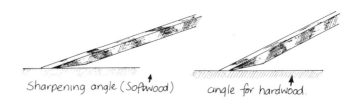

Sharpening angle (Softwood)   angle for hardwood.

The illustration shows two sharpening angles for chisels. The more acute angle is for cutting softwood. When chiselling hardwood you need a cutting edge with a steeper angle, which fractures and weakens the shavings to prevent the strong brittle shavings from controlling the tool. Chisels 'A' and 'A1' show how the tip of a well-sharpened blade should look. On chisel 'B', uneven hand pressure on the tool has ground the cutting edge unevenly. Sometimes the same fault is caused by a worn oilstone. Chisel 'C' will be hard to control. It will be difficult to shave or chop accurately, because the second bevel, on the back of the blade, prevents the back of the chisel from being steadied against the timber during the cut. Do not grind the back face of the chisel.

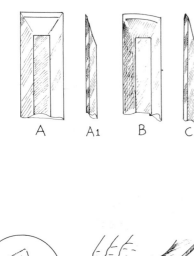

A   A1   B   C

■ Sharpening Procedure

Squirt a few drops of oil on the coarse grit sharpening stone. Hold the chisel and move it up and down the stone five or so times. Test for a burr by running your thumb down the back and over the edge of the blade. Continue grinding the edge in a parallel movement until a fine rough edge is felt at the very tip of the blade. Now press the back of the chisel flat on the stone, and with one or two sweeps remove the burr.

Repeat the process, pressing lightly, but keeping the chisel at exactly the same angle. Remove the burr and repeat for the third time.

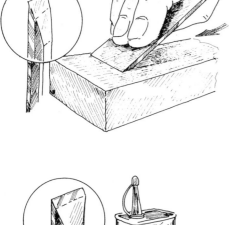

Using the fine grit oilstone, repeat this procedure. The blade will leave traces on the oilstone, revealing the condition of the edge. By watching the path of the blade you can tell when the notches have been ground out. Take a leather strop. You can make one from a scrap of leather belt, and smear it with sharpening compound which you can buy from a barber. Stroke the blade five times in one direction and once on its back. Repeat several times with diminished pressure. Watch the trail left by the blade in the compound. Fine parallel lines show that the blade is still too rough, and needs a little more grinding on the smooth stone. Keep the stropping ratio 5:1 to prevent a cutting angle developing on the back of the blade.

Planes

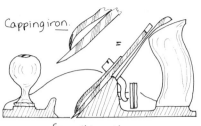
Capping iron.

Smoothing plane

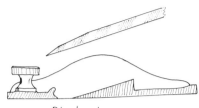
Block plane

Follow the same procedure as for sharpening chisels. The sharpening angles for the block plane and the smoothing plane are illustrated below. Note that on the smoothing plane blade a capping iron which braces the blade is clamped close to its cutting edge.

Saws

Saws do not need to be sharpened very often. It is time to service the blade when the saw bumps over the wood rather than cutting through it. Most tool shops provide a saw sharpening service, but unless the saw is badly damaged it is only half an hour's work to do the job yourself. In addition you will need a saw sharpening file and probably a saw set. Make up two simple saw cheeks to hold the blade steady.

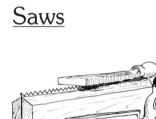

■ Filing

Arrange excellent lighting. Clamp the saw in the saw cheeks, leaving the teeth poking above its top. Run the saw file along the tips of the teeth. Every tooth should reflect light from the tiny flat filed on top. This reduces them all to the same height. Now take the saw file and, filing at right angles, file until each tooth is pointed. Take care when shaping the teeth: every file stroke shapes the back of one tooth and the front of the next, so irregularities have to be evened out; they cannot be removed by reshaping one tooth.

■ Setting

When all the teeth have been pointed, set them. This is necessary to allow the saw to slip easily through the wood. Try sawing through a scrap of wood. If the saw cuts evenly and does not bind, then miss this stage.

Adjust your saw setting tool to the number of teeth per 25 mm (1 in) on the sawblade and then, working one side at a time, pinch the teeth in the setter. Turn the blade round, and set the other side. Try out the saw. If the sawcut is too wide, lay the blade on its side and lightly run an oilstone down its teeth. Repeat on the other side and try sawing again. This should even out the set and reduce the sawcut.

■ Sharpening

Take the triangular file, start from the tip of the saw blade, and file alternate teeth in the direction illustrated. Three strokes per tooth should be sufficient. Repeat on the other side, using a fresh facet of the file, and the same number of strokes per tooth, and the saw is ready.

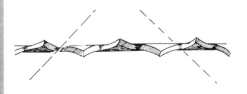
Each tooth has a point and two sharp edges.

ORCHARD BENCH

T HIS is a large piece of garden furniture which will seat four or five adults comfortably. In a small workshop it seems even bigger. It is quite a simple seat to make – the back is absolutely flat and all the seat supports, etc. are morticed straight into the back legs. There is a lot of repetitive work and it will help to have a powerful belt sander, electric hand planer, and electric all-purpose saw.

The back is made first. It is in five sections and has six legs, four short and two long, cut and shaped in pairs. The horizontal rails are tenoned into the legs, and the vertical back slats are tenoned into the rails. The front rails are morticed straight into the legs, except at the outer edges, where the tenons enter the legs at almost 45°. An unusual feature is the rim of wide covering boards, round the edge of the seat, to hold the seat slats. Note the front board is not grooved, and is a little wider than the side ones to compensate for the filling pieces inserted into the sides. In order to fit the seat slats, two front covering boards are fitted after the majority of the seat slats are in place.

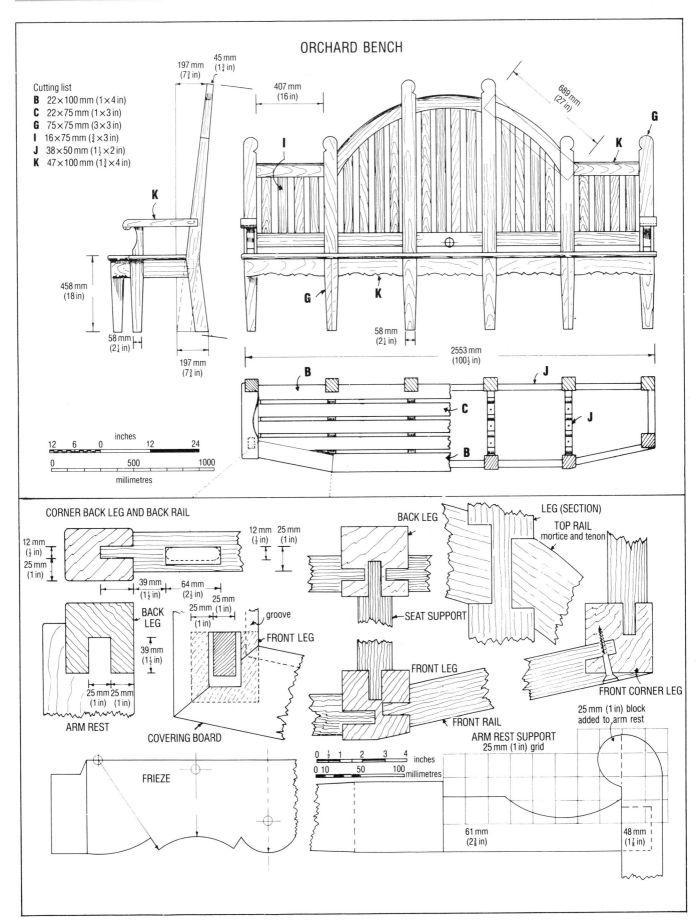

ORCHARD BENCH

Cutting list
B 22×100 mm (1×4 in)
C 22×75 mm (1×3 in)
G 75×75 mm (3×3 in)
I 16×75 mm (¾×3 in)
J 38×50 mm (1½×2 in)
K 47×100 mm (1¾×4 in)

197 mm (7¾ in)
45 mm (1¾ in)
407 mm (16 in)
689 mm (27 in)

458 mm (18 in)
58 mm (2¼ in)
197 mm (7¾ in)
58 mm (2¼ in)
2553 mm (100½ in)

inches
12   6   0   12   24
0   500   1000
millimetres

CORNER BACK LEG AND BACK RAIL

12 mm (½ in)
25 mm (1 in)
12 mm (½ in)
25 mm (1 in)
39 mm (1½ in)
64 mm (2½ in)
25 mm (1 in)

BACK LEG

39 mm (1½ in)
25 mm 25 mm (1 in) (1 in)

ARM REST

25 mm (1 in)
25 mm (1 in)
groove
FRONT LEG
COVERING BOARD

BACK LEG
SEAT SUPPORT

FRONT LEG
FRONT RAIL

LEG (SECTION)
TOP RAIL
mortice and tenon

FRONT CORNER LEG

FRIEZE

0   ½   1   2   3   4 inches
0 10   50   100 millimetres

ARM REST SUPPORT
25 mm (1 in) grid
25 mm (1 in) block
added to arm rest

61 mm (2⅜ in)
48 mm (1⅞ in)

23

Construction

Draw a full-size end elevation of the bench. Cut out the back legs, joining them at an angle and taper the top to 45 mm (1¾ in). Mark off the seat reference line, (the bottom of the seat rails), and then measure off and mark all the other mortices. Rout the mortices using the same fence setting, and a 12 mm (½ in) two-flute cutter.

■ Back Rails

Shape and glue the three curved back rails, clamping them tight with the string and wedges, as illustrated.

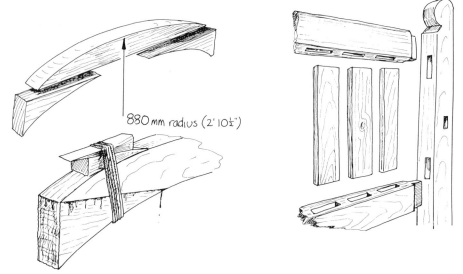

880 mm radius (2' 10½")

■ Backrest

Building one section at a time, tenon in the top and bottom rails, and then mark and cut out the mortices for the slats. Fit the slats, rounding their outer edges so that they drop easily into the mortices. Resting the legs on a large flat surface, and using pegs, use glue to fasten the back sections together. Sand the back when the glue is hard and the pegs have been trimmed off with a chisel.

■ Front Legs

Cut and shape the front and end legs. Cut out the stub tenons on the end legs, and mark and cut all the mortices on the middle four legs, but leave the front rail mortices on the two outside front legs.

■ Seat Supports

Make up all of the main seat supports, scalloping between the slats for drainage. Fit the front rails, tenoning them straight into the legs, and then jigsaw the frieze, or cut it out with the all-purpose saw, fitted with an 'S 427D' blade.

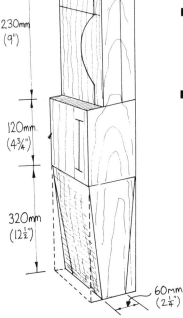

230mm
(9")

120mm.
(4¾")

320mm
(12½")

60mm
(2¼")

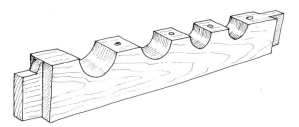

Armrests

Cut the tenon and lap joint for the two armrests, marking them in place. Trim them until they fit, then lower them over the stub tenons on the top of the front leg, and mark the position for the tenon on the armrests, see page 27. Check the positioning with a ruler before drilling out and chiselling the mortice square. When the armrests fit, saw them to shape, and glue the small block at the end of the armrest. Chisel and rasp this into shape once the glue has hardened.

Front Rails

Assemble the main seat framework, and cut out a cardboard template of the plan view of the two outside front rails. Include the two tenons; one is cut parallel with the face of the rail (the one at the outside corner), and the other is kinked slightly to enter the inner front legs at right angles. Now mark off and drill out the mortice in the side front legs, using a 12 mm (½ in) spade bit. Punch a few guide marks down the centre of the mortice with a hammer and nail point. Then, with the leg held fast in the vice, and holding the electric drill at the correct angle, drill a succession of holes down the mortice. Clear away the waste with a chisel. When the template fits into the mortice at the correct angle, and the shoulders at the opposite end meet up, mark and cut out the corner front rail, including the tenons, and fit them. Repeat on the other side, and then saw out the friezes on the underside.

Mortice centre line helps position drill.

Front corner leg

Seat Frame

Glue up the front seat assembly, including the armrests and all the front rails, holding the joints with pegs to pull them up tight. Glue up the four centre front legs and rails before glueing in the seat supports. When the latter are glued, check very carefully that the front legs align with the back.

Covering Board

Make a template for the two side covering boards. Cut out the boards and fit them, noting how the front corners are supported by the shoulders of the front leg. Rout a groove down the inside of the boards, and plane a radius around the outer front edge. Leave these two boards in position, and fit the next two boards, grooving the inside edge and rounding the outer edge as before, maintaining a constant overhang at the edge. Cut out the front covering board, which is a little wider than the side ones and does not need a groove at the inside edge, but round the front edge.

Glue and nail one pair of covering boards into position, and tack the opposite pair down, but make sure that you can remove them if you need to, by nailing through a thin block of plywood on top.

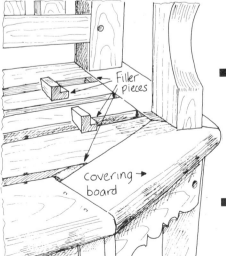

Filler pieces

covering board

Seat Slats

Now cut out, fit and glue the seat slats, glueing 25 mm (1 in) filler pieces between them into the groove in the covering board.

Glue and tack the second side covering board into position, and hammer it home when the first three slats are in place.

Fit the remaining slats and when all the joints are cut and ready, glue and fix them in position. Screw the slats and the seat supports from below.

Finishing

Treat all surfaces with wood preserver and stand the legs in plastic tubs half full of preservative for 3–4 minutes, to protect the end grain. When the preservative is completely dry, apply knotting to any knots and resinous crevices, then paint the chair with two coats of microporous white.

Marking out must be precise, and the chisel and saw cuts clean-edged. Arrange a good light to shine onto your work from the left (if you are right-handed), and sharpen your tools and marking knives. For advice on sharpening, see page 20.

Cross-Halving Joints

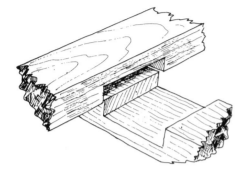

■ Marking Out

This joint can only be marked out and cut when the planks that are to be joined are at their finished dimensions. So, if there are marks or machining ripples to remove, plane them off first. Lay the pieces across each other at the correct angle, prick the corners where they intersect, with a knife, then draw in the joint with a pencil. Check their alignment before incising the pencil lines with a marking knife, starting the knife cut in the nicks already made, and bracing the knife against a set square or sliding bevel. Pencil in the waste parts of the joint, and then gauge in the depth of the slot in each part with a marking gauge. For pieces of equal thickness, the measurement will be the same.

Square off the sides with a pencil and a set square.

■ Cutting

Hold the first piece on the bench hook as illustrated, relieve the waste side of the line with a chisel, and saw down to the depth mark. Repeat at the other side of the joint, and, if it is a wide joint, at every clear 25 mm (1 in) of waste that needs removing. Never stray beyond the depth line.

■ Removing the Waste

Now use a very sharp 15 mm (⅝ in) chisel to pare away the waste wood. Shave down to the line on the first side, removing shavings no thicker than 1.5 mm (¹⁄₁₆ in) with each cut, then turn the wood around, and cut down to the line from the opposite side. The last cuts should start with the chisel lodged in the gauge line.

■ Assembly

Assemble very gently. It may be difficult to fit the two pieces together. If it is necessary to shave back an edge or two, mark them off with a knife before trimming with a chisel. Start the first cut in the middle of the joint, then work towards each side.

Mortice and Tenon Joint

Gauge marks

Shoulder

Tapered haunch

This is the main framing joint used in all of the projects in this book. Mortices are slots and are usually cut into the vertical members of the frame. The tenons or tongues are cut in the horizontal or joining members. The width of the mortice varies according to the individual stresses involved and the size of the pieces being joined. Where pieces being joined are of equal thickness, the width of the mortice or tenon should be equivalent to one third of the width of the wood. If the instructions in this book do not specify the width of the mortice, then one third the width of the piece being tenoned will be a safe guide. The length of the mortice is directly related to the overall height of the rail, but if the rail is jointed into the top of a leg, then the mortice will have to be shorter to prevent the tenon breaking out of the top. In this case a tapered haunch is cut to terminate the tenon at the top. If a panel groove runs out through the mortice, a square haunch that fills the groove is used instead.

Where two tenons meet and obstruct each other, a rough mitre is cut on the inside faces of the two tenons.

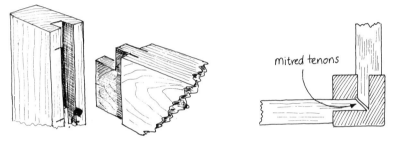

mitred tenons

■ Marking Out

Mark the mortice first. Draw in its length with a set square. If you do not have a mortice gauge with two scribers (one adjustable) set in its stock, scribe in the side nearest the face side with a marking gauge, and pencil in the other.

■ Cutting the Mortice

Using a routing box for stability, set the router to the correct depth, and the fence to the gauged setting, and plunge out the mortice. Start by routing two overlapping holes; alternate between them until the tool reaches to its full depth, and then work along the mortice, stopping on the pencil line marking the end of the mortice nearest to you. To clean up the mortice, run the router bit once or twice up and down the mortice, taking care at the ends. Tap out the mortice to remove the chips.

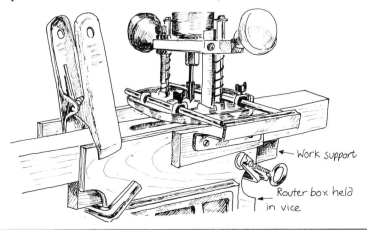

Work support

Router box held in vice

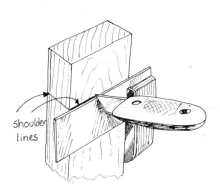

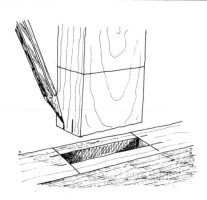

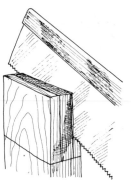

■ Tenon

The two important reference points for the tenon are the shoulder line, which defines the length of the rail, and the gauge line, which gives the offset for the tenon. Mark the shoulder with a set square, or sliding bevel if the shoulder is sloping, and incise the shoulder right around the rail. Use the marking gauge at its previous setting to scribe in the tenon offset and, holding the tenon in place, pencil in its other face. Saw down the cheeks, starting the sawcut at 45° into both lines and bringing the saw level as the cut is established. Cut with the leading point of the saw angled slightly downwards until the saw reaches the shoulder line. Stop at the shoulder line and cut the second face. Now turn the rail on its side and rest it on the bench hook. Chisel away a slither of waste from beside the line, then, lodging the saw in the shallow groove, hard up against the shoulder, cut off the tenon cheek. Repeat for the other side. Cut the haunch, and then trim the edges of the tenon until it fits neatly into the mortice.

Haunched Tenons

Mortices and tenons are cut as described above. Then saw, and chisel out, an angled wedge of wood from the top of the leg, using a suitable chisel. Measure off the height of the tenon and cut the haunch in it. A square haunch is measured and cut to fill an existing groove in the framework. Position the tenon so that it already fills the groove. The square haunch remains the width of the tenon, and the groove may need to be widened slightly with a chisel before it fits.

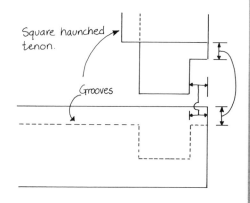

Pegged Mortices

Cut out the two parts of the joint as described on page 27. Insert some scrap wood into the mortice to stop it splitting, and drill a 9 mm (³⁄₈ in) hole through the centre of the mortice, from the face side, and out through the other side. Now push the tenon right in. Mark the tenon where the centre of the peg should be. If the peg is going to heave the tenon inwards, it will have to be off-centred slightly to the edge of the mortice. A 1.5 mm (¹⁄₁₆ in) offset is quite sufficient. Mark the centre for the hole in the tenon with a punch or nail. Withdraw the tenon. Support its underside on some scrap, and drill it with the 9 mm (³⁄₈ in) drill.

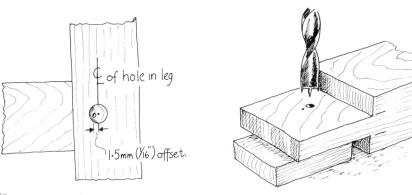

■ Cutting the Peg

Insert the tenon. Cut a 150 mm (6 in) length of 9 mm (³⁄₈ in) dowel, and taper one end with the bevel-edged chisel. Hammer in the temporary peg – it should pull the joint up tight.

■ Glueing Up

Make up enough temporary pegs for pulling all the joints in one operation. Knock out the pegs before the glue has set. Replace with hand-shaped pegs made from the same wood as the rest of the piece you are making. Trim their tops with a very sharp chisel held flat against the adjacent wood.

Mitre Joint

This joint is held together by a loose tongue slotted into both components of the joint. The angles of the mitres are dependent on the figure of the framework and the number of pieces being joined.

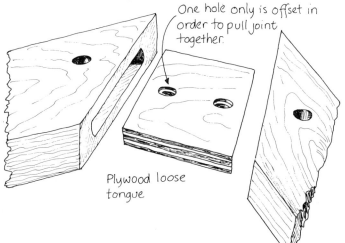

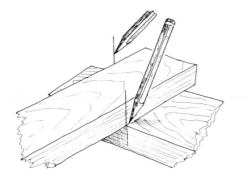

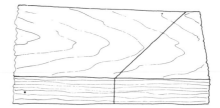

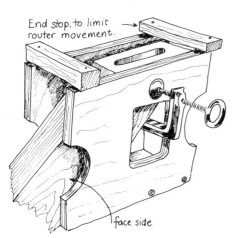

End stop, to limit router movement.

face side

Plywood Tenons

Stub Tenons

■ Marking Out

Set out the pieces to be joined, taking care to check that they are aligned correctly. Mark off the position for the mitres. Set the angle on the sliding bevel, mark off and square around with a set square. After checking that your marking-out is accurate and after pencilling in identification marks on the joints, saw each mitre, taking care not to undercut the joint. Plane the saw cut level with a block plane, or trim it with the router, fixing the work to a shooting board.

■ Routing the Mortice

Check that the mitres all fit together, then set up the router box to hold the work while it is being morticed. Nail blocks onto the top of the router box to prevent the router breaking out of the mortice, then plunge out the mortices in turn. Keep the router fence setting, but change the router box set-up when the opposite ends of the planks are being routed.

Cut a cardboard template for the loose tenon, then cut it from 9 mm (³⁄₈ in) exterior or marine grade plywood, or a straightgrained wood offcut. Glue and peg one half of the tenon, then drill, and mark up the second half for pulling up with a peg.

■ Marking Out

Mark off the stub tenon and mark in the shoulders with a set square and marking knife.

■ Sawing

Saw down the tenon, working round the leg, and stopping the saw cut at the shoulder line. Now, saw the cheeks, keeping just to the waste side of the shoulder line. Trim the shoulders, starting at the

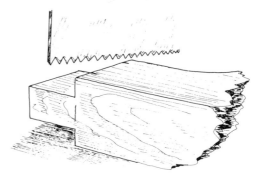

centre of each shoulder line. Lodge the 9 mm (⅜ in) chisel in the incised shoulder line, and chop straight downwards, slightly undercutting the shoulder. Still keeping in the line, move the chisel along the line and, with a rocking motion, eat away the waste until you reach the very corner of the wood. Here, you chisel straight down, taking your direction of cut from the shoulder line on the new face. Snip off the corners last, checking that the chisel follows both marking lines, leaving a perfectly square corner to the stub tenon. Repeat for the other three sides.

■ Marking the Mortice

For all the joins in this book it is possible to hold the piece almost exactly in position over the stub tenon, to draw round it. Check the dimensions after doing this, then square up the mortice with a set square. Drill out the centre of the mortice, pre-setting the depth stop so that the drill does not bite right through the wood. Chop out the mortice with the 15 mm (⅝ in) bevel-edged chisel, tapping it lightly on the handle with a mallet if necessary.

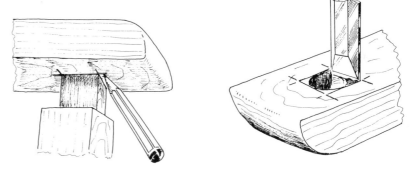

Angled Mortice and Tenon Joints

These joints are no more difficult to make than standard mortice and tenon joints described on page 26, but they are tricky to mark out. In some, the mortice is cut square to the face of the chair leg, and the tenon is cut at an angle to the rail 'A'. In other cases, where the wood is weaker, the mortice is cut at a slant, and the tenon is cut straight, with only its shoulders trimmed at an angle 'B'.

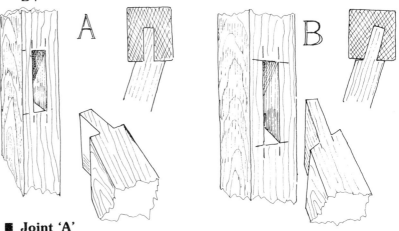

■ Joint 'A'

Draw out a full-size plan of the joint, making sure that the components are in their correct alignment relative to each other. If it is the seat of a chair, draw the entire seat plan, including the four legs and the front and back rails, full-size.

■ Marking the Tenon

Mark out and cut the mortice as for a normal joint. Now take dimensions and angles from the full-sized plans and mark in the shoulder line for the tenon, and the depth of the offset for the face of the tenon at the shoulder. Mark off the width of the tenon by referring to the mortice. From the plans, mark in the angled shoulder line on the top of the horizontal rail (with a sliding bevel) and the tenon, which should be square to it. Check these lines by holding the horizontal rail in its correct position relative to the vertical member, and placing a parallel-sided card or wood offcut onto the rail. Pencil along its edge where it crosses the rail. This line should be parallel to the angled tenon face marked off on the top of the rail. Check the offset with dividers.

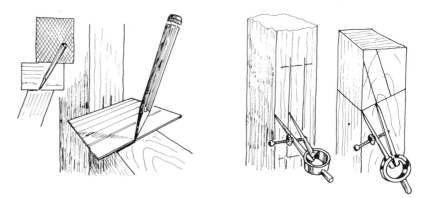

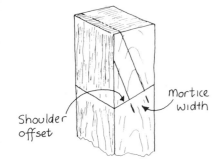

Shoulder offset

Mortice width

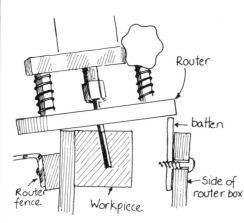

Router

batten

Side of router box

Router fence

Workpiece

Insert tenon, adjust the line, then trim the shoulder to the line.

■ Cutting the Tenon

Now cut out the tenon, making sure not to cut too close to the shoulder line. Insert the tenon and check the angles of the shoulder, then trim the shoulder to the line, nibbling back the waste until there is a perfect joint.

■ Joint 'B'

The angled mortice avoids having to cut the tenon across the line of the grain.

■ Using the Router Box

Set up the router box, taking the angle of the mortice from the plans. Set the angle using the sliding bevel, and elevate one side of the router box with a batten, which you can screw on with a pair of self-tapping screws.

■ Fitting the Rail

The tenon is cut straight, and parallel to the side of the rail. The angle of the shoulders can be taken from the drawings, or they can be marked once the tenon cheeks are cut, when the tenon is inserted into the mortice. Transfer the angle with a ruler or parallel batten. Shave away the face of the shoulder with a sharp chisel until it fits perfectly.

MAKING DECORATIVE CHAIR BACKS

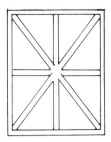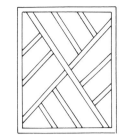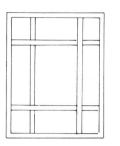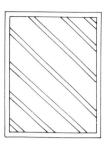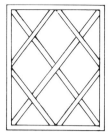

The decorative backs illustrated are made inside a battened framework and fitted into the seat as a complete unit. The joints used in constructing the back are shown below. It is not difficult to make a decorative back, provided that it is built in stages, and you allow plenty of time for the glue to harden between stages.

A variety of designs has been suggested and is illustrated here. The instructions below will enable you to make any of them, or to construct patterns of your own design.

Cross-halving: for making good joints you must have extremely sharp tools – a scalpel or a very sharp hobby knife will be ideal for incising the marking lines, use sharp chisels to relieve the waste side of the line prior to sawing and a very sharp block plane for

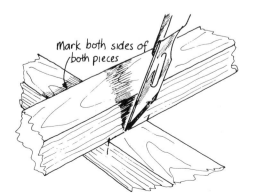

Mark both sides of both pieces

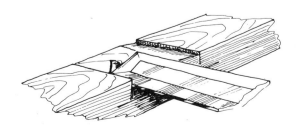

shaving the mitres. You will also need a fine saw. If you do not have a dovetail saw, which has about sixteen teeth per 25 mm (1 in), fit a fresh blade to a hack saw, and use it instead. Trim the joint using a chisel with vertical guillotine chopping motion, and use the block plane in conjunction with a cutting board, to cut mitres and scarfs accurately.

Use either thixotropic epoxy resin or, if the chair is to be painted, resorcinol resin (which is cheaper and easier to use).

Construction

Construct the chair back on a flat board with the full scale pattern marked on it.

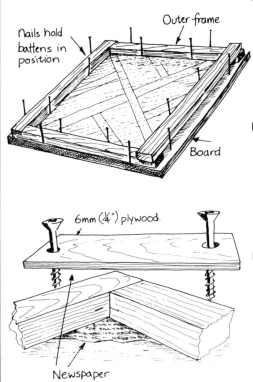

Nails hold battens in position

Outer frame

Board

■ First Stage

Make the outside frame first. Cut the battens to length and position them on the board, holding them in place against nails driven into the board. Saw the cross-halving joints, and glue them together on the board, clamping them with the simple strap clamp illustrated. Prevent the joints from adhering to the board or clamp with scraps of newspaper.

■ Second Stage

Remove the outer frame from the board, and mark the front face on it. Now, cut battens for the decorative pattern. Note from the accompanying drawings the shape of each joint. These backs are not strong, and the joints must be either properly lapped or scarfed to give an adequate glued surface area. A simple butt joint or short scarf will break.

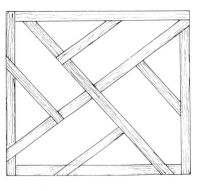

6mm (¼") plywood.

Newspaper

■ Third Stage

(For stained and varnished work only). Decide on the relative prominence of the struts. At each halving joint, for instance, one of the two pieces seems continuous, and the other will appear to make way for it. In the examples below I have shown two alternative appearances for the same back. One is more satisfying than the other, because the manner of cutting the joints has enhanced the rhythm of the pattern. Pencil onto the battens the waste parts of each joint.

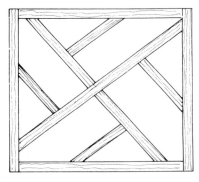

Fourth Stage

Guided by the full-size pattern drawn on the board, and holding the battens with nails as shown, mark the joints, and cut the rear facing parts. Then cut the forward-facing shoulders, which are easier to mark now that the first halving provides some stability to the joint.

Fifth Stage

Glue together the first struts, holding the joints with the strap clamps. Wait for the glue to try, then continue to build up the back.

Sixth Stage

When the inner work is finished, lay the outer frame over the decorative part and sink it flush, again cutting the rear-facing shoulders first. Clean up the work, trim the outer edges of the frame, and slide it into place. Now glue it in position, and wipe away excess glue. Fill any cracks with epoxy resin or a weatherproof filler, and sand it smooth with an orbital sander.

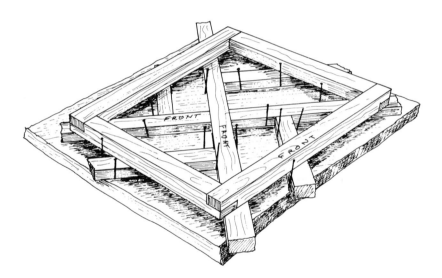

GARDEN CHAIR

THIS is a simple chair to construct, and it is easy to arrange your tools and workshop schedule to make several in one go. Although the proportions of the chair are graceful, heavy pieces of wood are used in its construction. The legs are cut from 50 mm (2 in) square section, spliced as described on page 44. The side, front and back rails are morticed into the legs. Apart from the shoulders on the front and back rails, which are at right angles, all the others are cut out of square. Even the joint between the front leg and the side rail is sloping.

The seat is made from slats, 18 mm (¾ in) thick, nailed and glued to the rails. Along the front and between the back legs, pieces are glued into the gaps between the slats to conceal and protect the rails, and form an unbroken edge.

The crest rail is sawn from a single wide board, and is morticed to hold the three back slats.

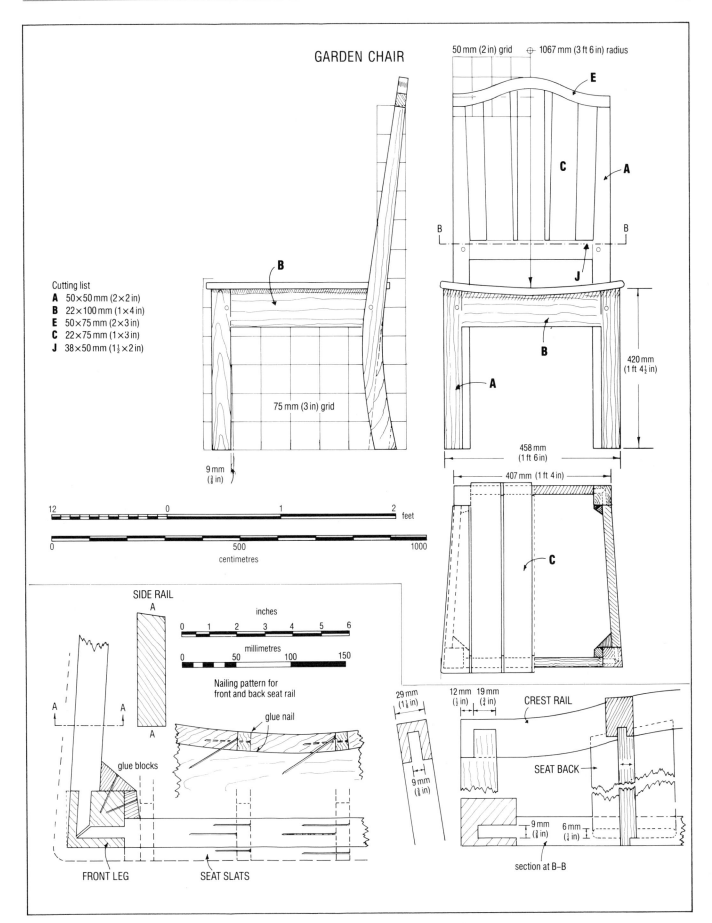

GARDEN CHAIR

50 mm (2 in) grid ⊕ 1067 mm (3 ft 6 in) radius

E

B

C

A

B   B

J

Cutting list
A 50×50 mm (2×2 in)
B 22×100 mm (1×4 in)
E 50×75 mm (2×3 in)
C 22×75 mm (1×3 in)
J 38×50 mm (1½×2 in)

B

A

420 mm
(1 ft 4½ in)

75 mm (3 in) grid

458 mm
(1 ft 6 in)

9 mm
(⅜ in)

12   0   1   2 feet

0   500   1000
centimetres

407 mm (1 ft 4 in)

C

SIDE RAIL
A

inches
0 1 2 3 4 5 6

millimetres
0 50 100 150

Nailing pattern for
front and back seat rail

glue nail

A   A

A

glue blocks

FRONT LEG   SEAT SLATS

29 mm
(1⅛ in)

12 mm
(½ in)

19 mm
(¾ in)

CREST RAIL

SEAT BACK

9 mm
(⅜ in)

9 mm
(⅜ in)

6 mm
(¼ in)

section at B–B

Construction

■ Back Legs

Draw a full-sized end elevation of the chair.

Mark out the back legs, cut them to shape and splice and glue them as described on page 44. Saw and plane the tapers at the top of the back legs, and smooth them with a belt sander. Avoid sanding the areas where there will be joints. Hold the legs together and mark off the mortices and the stub tenons at the tops. Saw the stub tenons, leaving some scope for adjustment at the shoulders. Rout out the middle and back rail mortices. Set the side of the router box to the correct elevation and rout out the side rail mortices, as described on page 27. Leave the router box at this setting as it will be useful when routing the front legs. Plane the inside taper from just above the middle rail.

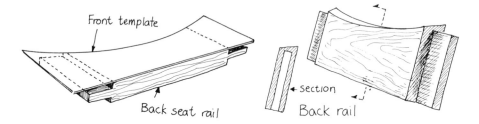

Front template

Back seat rail

← section

Back rail

■ Back Rails

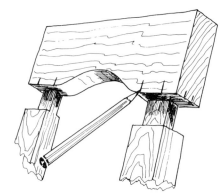

Make a cardboard template of the curve at the top of the front rail. The back seat rail is shorter than the front rail, but they are both cut from the same width of wood, so place the template at the centre of the back rail, running it out as illustrated, and pencil it in. Mark off the shoulders and saw the tenons before cutting the curve with a jigsaw, and bevelling the curve, as illustrated. Cut out and fit the middle rail, morticing the slots for the backrest. When both rails are fitted, assemble the back, and mark off on the crest-rail blank the position of the mortices for the two stub tenons. Rout these out and fit them, trimming the shoulders until they fit perfectly. Now saw the inner curve of the back rail. Mark off and rout the slots for the backrest, which can be fitted now, and glue down the crest rail or leave the back until later and leave it unglued until it has been fitted, (see page 30). Glue and peg the back rail assembly, then sand.

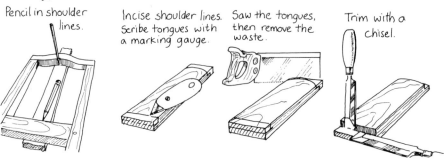

Pencil in shoulder lines.

Incise shoulder lines. Scribe tongues with a marking gauge.

Saw the tongues, then remove the waste.

Trim with a chisel.

■ Front Legs

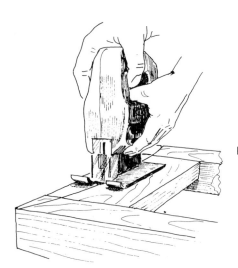

Mortice the front legs. The front rail enters the legs at right-angles, but the side rail mortices are plunged out at the same angle as those at the back. Note the side rail mortices are inset slightly to allow for the angle of the seat rails. Saw the tenons and fit the front rail. Now draw the curve across the top of the rail and legs and saw it off with a jigsaw.

■ Side Rails

Fit the side rails into the back legs, and fit the other end into the front legs, trimming the shoulders until they fit. Note that the vertical shoulders at each end of the side rail are cut at an angle, which can be lifted from the full-sized elevation of the side. When the side rails fit, plane down the outer edges of the front legs until they are flush with the outer edge of the side rail. Correct the angle at the top of the rail to match the curve cut in the tops of the front legs, so that the seat slats can be glued down.

■ Fitting the Seat

Glue the chair together, pulling the joints tight with pegs. Glue corner blocks between the rails, notching them to nestle against the legs. Cut the seat slats 25 mm (1 in) longer than you need. Fit them at the edges first, then fit in the remainder of the seat slats, glueing them and nailing them with stainless steel panel pins, and leaving an air gap of 6 mm (¼ in) between the slats. Fit the wedge-sectioned filling pieces, pressing them between the slats to a line pencilled 3 mm (⅛ in) inside the back and front rails.

When the glue has dried, trim the overhangs at the front and back, plane a small radius on the edge of the seat and at the corners.

Fill all the holes, treat the chair with preservative, then paint it with microporous paint or woodstain.

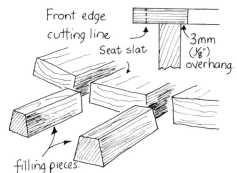

Front edge
cutting line
Seat slat
3mm (⅛") overhang.
filling pieces.

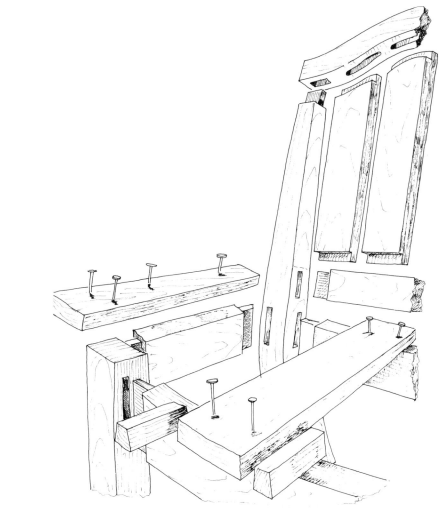

ARMCHAIR

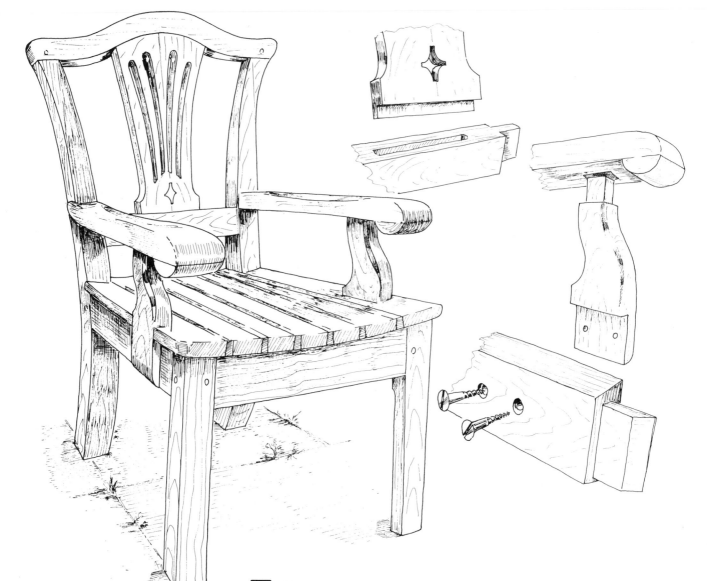

Tʜɪs is a simple and elegant armchair. The style is similar to that of the single chairs described on the previous pages. In this example a single shaped splat decorates the backrest and provides support. As can be seen from the drawings, this armchair is slightly wider than the single chairs, and the wood sections for the front and back legs are heavier. The armrest supports are screwed and glued to the side rails, and the armrests are tenoned into the back legs and morticed onto the stub tenons of the armrest supports. Because of the heavier sections of wood used in this chair, pare away unnecessary wood to lighten its appearance. Radius the backs of the upper legs and the back of the crest rail, and chamfer the inside corners of the front legs. Note that the slight angle to the front legs, shown in the side elevation, helps to lighten this design.

If you are making two armchairs and a set of singles, the back patterns are interchangeable, although some slight alterations in size are needed to keep the patterns in proportion.

ARMCHAIR

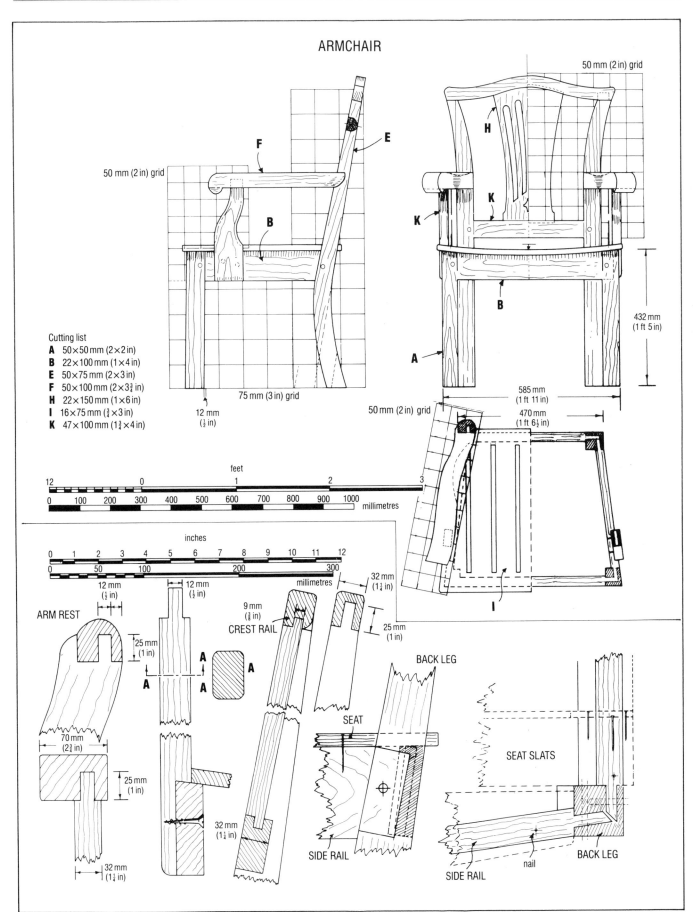

50 mm (2 in) grid

50 mm (2 in) grid

F

E

B

H

K

K

B

A

B

432 mm
(1 ft 5 in)

585 mm
(1 ft 11 in)

470 mm
(1 ft 6½ in)

50 mm (2 in) grid

I

75 mm (3 in) grid

12 mm
(½ in)

Cutting list
A 50×50 mm (2×2 in)
B 22×100 mm (1×4 in)
E 50×75 mm (2×3 in)
F 50×100 mm (2×3¾ in)
H 22×150 mm (1×6 in)
I 16×75 mm (¾×3 in)
K 47×100 mm (1¾×4 in)

feet
12   0   1   2   3
0 100 200 300 400 500 600 700 800 900 1000
millimetres

inches
0 1 2 3 4 5 6 7 8 9 10 11 12
0   50   100   200   300
millimetres

12 mm
(½ in)

12 mm
(½ in)

9 mm
(⅜ in)

32 mm
(1¼ in)

25 mm
(1 in)

CREST RAIL

ARM REST

25 mm
(1 in)

A
A
A
A

A

A

BACK LEG

70 mm
(2¾ in)

25 mm
(1 in)

32 mm
(1¼ in)

SEAT

32 mm
(1¼ in)

SIDE RAIL

SEAT SLATS

BACK LEG

SIDE RAIL

nail

Construction

For additional guidance turn to the Single Chair on page 36.

Draw a full-sized end elevation of this chair, taking the dimensions and angles from the plans.

■ Legs

Cut out the back legs, join them into the curves as described on page 44 and mark the height line for the shoulders of the stub tenons, and the positions of the back leg mortices. Rout out all of the mortices except those for the side rails, which will be cut at an angle.

Draw out a full-sized elevation of the front legs and, from this, mark up and cut out a cardboard template of the curve of the front rail. Use this to mark off the top edge of the back seat rail. Now cut and fit the back seat and middle rails.

When these fit, cut out the curve on the top edge of the back seat rail, and bevel the curve at the angle shown in the side elevation for the seat slats. Now mark off the taper for the insides of the back legs, and plane them to the line.

Assemble the back legs, drawing up the mortices with pegs, and mark in the shoulderline for the crest rail with a straightedge. Cut out the crest rail, and shape the curved underside, cut out the stub tenons on the legs, and mortice the crest rail to fit, as described on page 36.

■ Backsplat

The backsplat fits into a shallow groove in the crest rail, and into a similar slot in the middle rail, where it is left unglued so that it can swell and shrink with changes in humidity.

Cut out the grooves using a 6 mm (¼ in) two-flute router cutter, setting it in 6 mm (¼ in) from the front edges of the crest and the middle rails. The grooves should be central and slightly shorter than the overall width of the backsplat.

Now choose a quarter-sawn piece of 12 mm (½ in) wood for the back splat. You can tell if it is quarter-sawn by inspecting the endgrain pattern at the top of the plank. The plank you need should have a straight grain, with perpendicular growth rings at the ends, as illustrated. Make a template of the back splat, and then cut it out, remembering to add 12 mm (½ in) extra at each end for the tongues which hold it in place. Cut the bottom rebate first, and fit the splat into the middle rail. When you are satisfied that the lower joint is good, rout out, or trim with a chisel the major part of the upper rebate. Then scribe in the curved shoulder which abuts the crest rail, as illustrated, before finishing the jointing with a chisel.

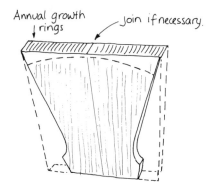

Annual growth rings

Join if necessary.

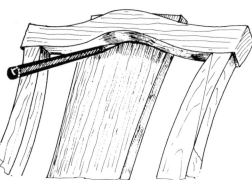

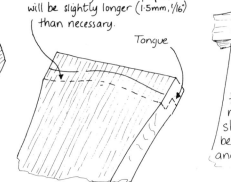

Preliminary shoulder, splat will be slightly longer (1·5mm, ¹⁄₁₆") than necessary.

Tongue

When the splat is held at the top by the crest rail mortice, the shoulder line can be marked again and trimmed.

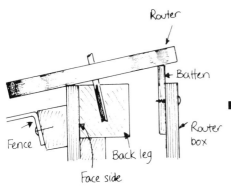

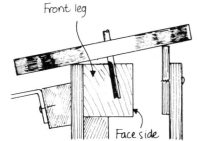

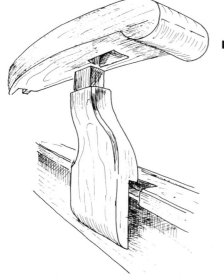

When the splat blank is fitting neatly at the top and the bottom, and the stub tenons holding the crest rail are closed up tightly, cut out the outline of the splat, and the pierced decorations. For pierced work, drill through the waste parts of the pattern, and then poke the jigsaw blade into the hole to begin the sawcut.

■ Front Legs

Cut the front legs to length, mark off and rout out the mortices for the front rail. Cut out the front rail, fit the tenons, and then, with the parts assembled, cut the front curve.

Draw out a full-scale plan of the seat and lift from it the angles at which the side rails converge on the back and front legs.

Now set up the router box, elevating one side so that the router can cut out the side rail mortices. Mark the ends of the front leg with the angle for the mortice, before routing them out, to enable you to check the angles.

While the router box is out, cut out the side rail mortices for the back legs, keeping the angle the same, but slightly altering the fence adjustment to accommodate the differences as illustrated.

■ Side Rails

Cut out the side rails, including sufficient for the tenons at each end. Mark off the tenons, taking the vertical shoulder angles from the full-size side elevation, and the converging angles from the full-sized plan of the seat. Fit the side rails, adjusting the tenons and mortices as necessary. When both sides are fitting, mark off on their top edge the angle at which it will have to be trimmed to hold the seat slats, and plane them to the angle, (see page 31).

Assemble the chair and, if necessary, adjust the tops of the seat rails so that the seat slats can be fitted easily. Now trim the chair back, and champher the inside corners of the front legs as mentioned above before assembling and glueing up the chair.

■ Armrests

Draw the plan view of the armrests onto the full-sized plan of the seat and make a template from its outline. Cut the armrests, saw and fit the joints into the back legs. Complete the shaping of the armrest with a jigsaw, files and rasps. Now cut and fit the two supports, and saw the stub tenons. Then counterbore and screw the armrests to the side rails. Lower the armrests over the supports and mark off the positions for the mortices. When they fit, glue them in position, holding the armrests tight with a pair of beams and tourniquets.

Fill any remaining holes and crevices, and sand the chair smooth. Finish with microporous paint.

■ Seat

Cut and fit the seat slats, starting at the corners, and working towards the centre. Fit the wedge-shaped filling pieces before the glue cures, aligning them with a pencil line drawn across the front and back rails. Trim the front and back edges and round all four sides after the glue has cured, then fill the nail holes with weatherproof filler. Sand the filler smooth.

MARKING OUT, SHAPING AND GLUEING CURVED COMPONENTS

These instructions feature the curved back legs of the chairs and benches described in this book, but the techniques described will also help in shaping and glueing other components needed for these projects.

■ Drawing Out

First make a cardboard template. Even if you are only making a single curved piece, it will help to have a template so that you arrive at the exact shape before you mark on the wood. Take some light card, long and wide enough for the back leg, and draw the 75 mm (3 in) grid on it. Refer to the plans and mark off where the line of the leg intersects with a grid line. Check your work thoroughly, before joining up the marks on your grid with a pencil line using a straightedge for the straights, and a bent batten, or french curves cut freehand from cardboard offcuts for the rest. Mark on the template the exact positions of the joint reference line, the mortices and the tenon shoulders. Cut out the template with a sharp knife held at a low angle.

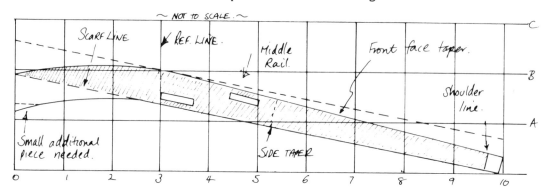

~ NOT TO SCALE. ~

SCARF LINE · REF. LINE. · Middle Rail · Front face taper. · C · B · Shoulder line. · A · Small additional piece needed. · SIDE TAPER

0 1 2 3 4 5 6 7 8 9 10

■ Marking Out

Take the template, position it carefully on the wood, and pencil round it. Mark on the reference line and all the joints.

■ Cutting Out

Use the electric jigsaw for cutting stock up to 50 mm (2 in) thick. Engage the orbital cutting action if your jigsaw has one, as it helps the blade cut quickly and accurately. Apply minimum horizontal pressure to the saw, so the blade is not pressed too quickly into the wood. If you work too fast, the sawblade will bend and its tip will wander off the line. For cutting the thicker bench legs, you will need a bandsaw or a multi-purpose saw (see page 12). Attach a hooked blade to help draw the saw through the wood, and use light forward pressure.

■ Glueing

Position the offcuts to complete the curve of the leg. Take an old hacksaw blade, and roughen the two glueing surfaces. The problem with glueing together two tapered pieces is that, lubricated by the glue, they slip apart when you clamp them together. Before clamping you will have to trap a dowel between

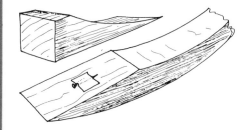

them to provide a positive location. Mark the dowel centres with a sewing pin, placing the head where you want the dowel hole. Tape it to the glueing face. Press the second piece against it, and the indents left by the head in both pieces are the centre points for the dowel. Use a brad point, or a spade bit drill which has spurs at its edge, for drilling the two 9 mm (⅜ in) holes. If you are drilling freehand, watch the circumference marks scored by the drill. The drill will be more or less perpendicular to the glueing face, if the spurs are cutting evenly around the centre point. Cut a short length of dowel to fit between the two pieces, lay some newspaper on a flat table and, resting the leg on the paper, glue and press the joint together. Fit a clamp across the joint and, with two blocks to prevent bruising the work with the clamp, tighten it up.

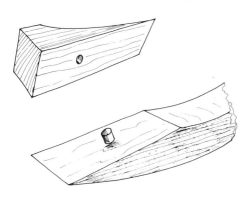

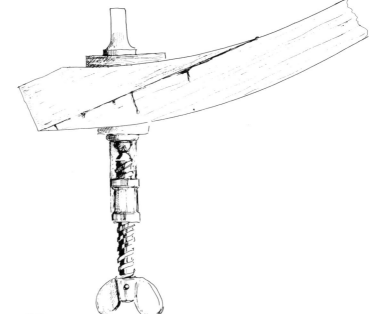

■ Smoothing

Smooth the convex shapes with a plane. Use the block plane for the concave curves, holding it at an angle where the curve is tight. Finish with the belt sander mounted on the bench, (see page 14), using the roller at the front of the sander to work into the tighter parts.

CONVERSATION CHAIR

THIS is an interesting and challenging piece of furniture to make. The serpentine back is formed in sections made from long thin pieces of pine, bent and glued together. Beneath it, a similarly curved beam forms the main part of the seat framework, into which the vertical back slats are morticed. There are 17 back slats, each one shaped with a router.

This is quite a lightly constructed seat, which gains strength from the girder formed by the upper and lower back rail. Note that the seat slats are rebated into grooves in the seat frame, and the back splats are morticed into the laminated serpentine framework. The front edges of the seat slats rest on the two straight frame rails.

A lot of preparation is required before the parts are glued and jointed together. This early work must be accurate. Laminating, in particular, is a messy job, and it is important that all the work is thoughtfully set up and carefully controlled. There have to be enough clamps to hold the wood, and the board onto which the mould blocks are bolted must be well fixed down and strong enough to withstand the forces imposed in the bending. Once the glue has hardened, it is vital that the laminated components are trimmed accurately. With firm dimensional control, marking up and jointing will be straightforward.

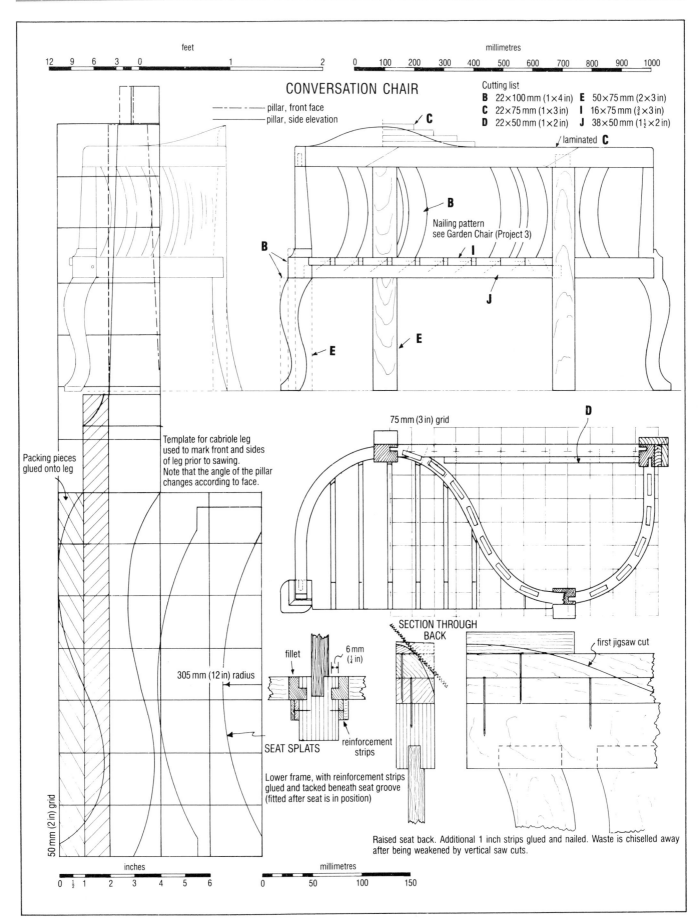

feet

12 9 6 3 0 1 2

millimetres

0 100 200 300 400 500 600 700 800 900 1000

CONVERSATION CHAIR

— · — pillar, front face
——— pillar, side elevation

Cutting list
B 22×100 mm (1×4 in) **E** 50×75 mm (2×3 in)
C 22×75 mm (1×3 in) **I** 16×75 mm (¾×3 in)
D 22×50 mm (1×2 in) **J** 38×50 mm (1½×2 in)

C

laminated C

B

Nailing pattern
see Garden Chair (Project 3)

B

I

J

E

E

Packing pieces
glued onto leg

Template for cabriole leg
used to mark front and sides
of leg prior to sawing.
Note that the angle of the pillar
changes according to face.

75 mm (3 in) grid

D

305 mm (12 in) radius

50 mm (2 in) grid

fillet

6 mm
(¼ in)

SEAT SPLATS

reinforcement
strips

Lower frame, with reinforcement strips
glued and tacked beneath seat groove
(fitted after seat is in position)

SECTION THROUGH
BACK

first jigsaw cut

Raised seat back. Additional 1 inch strips glued and nailed. Waste is chiselled away
after being weakened by vertical saw cuts.

inches

0 ½ 1 2 3 4 5 6

millimetres

0 50 100 150

Construction

■ Cutting out the Shaped Splats

There are 17 identical splats. They are cut from 100 mm × 25 mm (4 in × 1 in) pine, and each one is profiled at the edge. If you do not have a router bench, make up a router box, and after fitting the template guide for steering the router, measure the offset for the template, then saw and smooth the template edges. The retaining blocks screwed to the router box fit tightly against the wood which is to be shaped into the back splats, and hold the wood steady while the router is shaping its edges.

When the router box is ready, screw it to the work bench. Cut all the splats to length using the right-angle slide and a depth stop on the cutter saw for total accuracy. Press the first splat into place and cover it with the template, locating the template onto the two stub dowels of the router box. Use a 6 mm (¼ in) two-flute cutter to carve out the curve on each side of the splat. Repeat for the remaining splats, then sand.

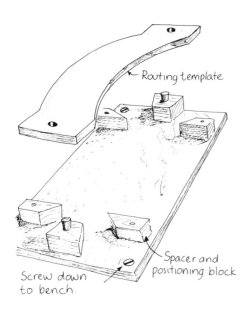

Routing template

Screw down to bench.

Spacer and positioning block

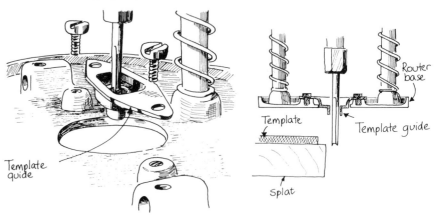

Template guide

Template guide

Template

Template guide

Router base

Splat

■ Laminating

The next stage is to laminate the two 'S' shaped components. Choose wood that is knot-free and with an open straight grain running parallel to the edge of the plank. Discontinuities in the grain will either fracture when the wood is bent, or will bend unevenly. Select enough pieces for the upper and lower framework, and saw them into strips 4.5 mm (³⁄₁₆ in) wide. Leave the slight surface roughness left by the circular saw blade – the fine ridges help the glue to sink into the wood.

The serpentine curve is made from three separate pieces. The two end pieces 'A' are identical, and the 'S' shaped middle section 'B' is symmetrical. In the lower framework, the sections are joined into the legs, but in the upper framework the sections overlap each other, and are joined with a sloping scarf joint. Two moulds will be needed, one for the four end pieces, and one for

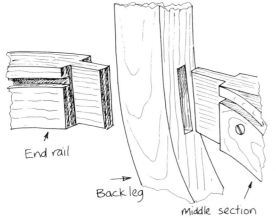

End rail

Back leg

middle section

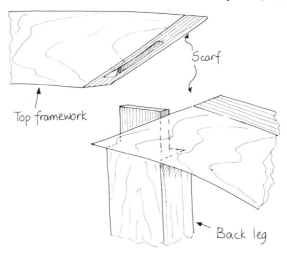

Scarf

Top framework

Back leg

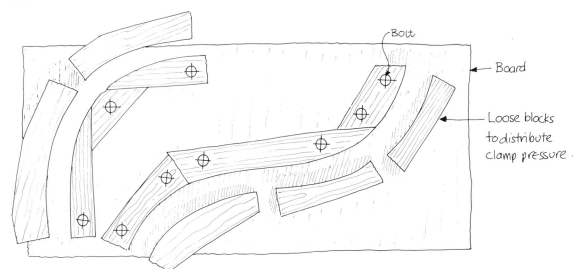

Bolt

Board

Loose blocks to distribute clamp pressure.

Newspaper

the two centre sections. Cut out the moulds from sturdy blocks with a jigsaw or all purpose saw, and bolt them onto a flat board onto which you have drawn the curves. Now assemble enough clamps to hold the longest (central) section of the moulds together while the glue is curing; do not start laminating unless you are sure you have enough clamps. You will need at least six 'G' clamps. If necessary, make up some as illustrated on page 64.

Once the mould is made, and you are certain you have enough clamps, begin laminating. Begin with the lower framework. Place newspaper over the laminating board, and glue and clamp up the strips. It is not possible to guarantee that there will be continuous contact between each piece however many clamps are used, so apply lots of glue. The glue will help lubricate the strips as they slide against each other, and any residue that does not squeeze onto the newspaper and all over your hands will fill the voids in the laminate. Remember not to overtighten the clamps – there should be enough pressure to close the gaps, but not so much that there is no glue left in the joint.

Wash off surplus glue with a rag before leaving it to cure. When the work is released, make the next component, and plane up the one you have just glued. When all the pieces have been laminated and cleaned up, groove the bottom framework with a router.

■ Cutting the Joints

Cut out the four legs, mortice them, and cut the stub tenons at their tops. Use a template to find the correct angle for the tenons and shoulder for the two end rails, cut and fit them. Select straight-grained pine for the main rails, and tenon them into the legs. Note that this rail is 25 mm (1 in) shallower than the laminated sections.

■ Seat Frame

Assemble the basic framework of the seat, and check the ends for squareness by measuring diagonals. Tack some nails and battens between the two rails to hold them, and plane up and fit the 'S' shaped diagonal. Mark off the angles at the ends so that the curves meld into each other. After checking that the 'S' member smoothly completes the serpentine curve, and the bottom of its groove is level with the top of the main straight members, glue and screw the 'B' diagonal in place.

■ Back Mortices

Mark off the positions for the slat mortices in the lower rail, cut them out with the router, then glue and peg together the ends 'A', the legs, and the two rails and diagonal 'B'.

■ Seat Slats

Fit the seat slats. Transfer the curve of the back with a pair of dividers, and chisel out the short tongue to fit into the framework groove. Glue the front edges to the straight rail. Fit filling pieces as you go, and trim the front edges when the glue is dry.

■ Top Rail

Laminate the top rail, allowing 200 mm (8 in) excess at each end of the serpentine part for the scarf joints that join the end pieces 'A' to the centre piece 'B'. Mortice in the legs, and then mark and scarf together the three back sections, taking care that the armrest curves mirror those of the seat framework below.

■ Back Slats

Now, with the backrest in position, mark off the positions for the back slats in the upper laminated frame. Plunge out the mortices, fit the slats, and glue up the backrest, tensioning it with tourniquets tied around the lower frame.

■ Capping Piece

Clean up and fit the capping piece, and round off all the corners before finishing the chair.

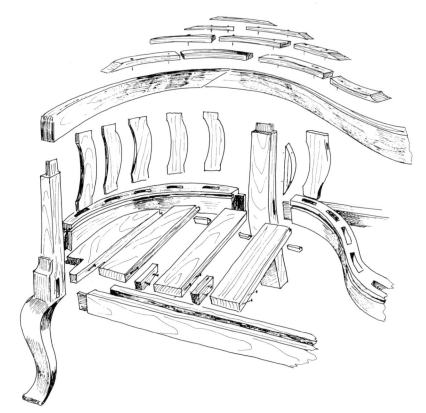

SCARFING

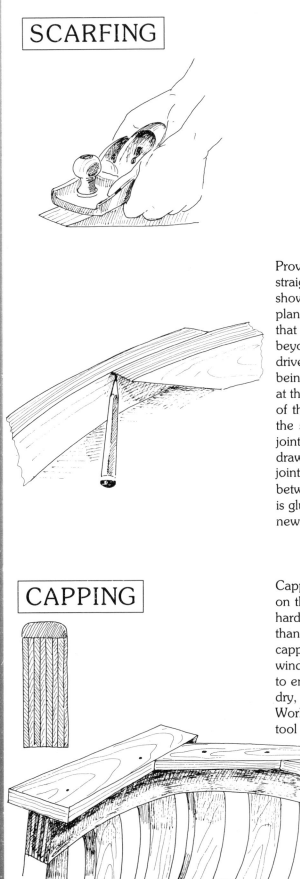

Pressure point at the finish of the stroke

Pressure point at the start of the stroke

Provided that the glued surface area is sufficiently large, the straight scarf is a very strong joint. Cut one component at the angle shown, and plane it smooth, taking great care not to rock the block plane when doing so. To work to this kind of accuracy, make sure that the blade is extremely sharp, with a bare minimum projecting beyond the sole of the plane. Hold the plane with two hands, and drive it forward. Let your fingers bear against the sides of the piece being levelled to guide it. Press the front of the plane downwards at the start of the stroke, then as the front begins to ride off the end of the scarf, press the back. Check that the scarf is flat by resting the sole of the smoothing plane on it. Transfer the angle of the joint to the second piece by laying both parts on a flat board, then draw from one onto the other, and cut and trim that too. Make the joint as described on page 44 inserting a 9 mm (³⁄₈ in) dowel between the two pieces to prevent the joint slipping apart when it is glued. Clamp it flat down onto a board protected with a sheet of newspaper.

CAPPING

Capping pieces are fitted last to hide the lines of the laminations on the upper edge of the armrest. Cut them from pine, or from a harder wearing hardwood. Fit them in short lengths, not longer than 45 cm (18 in), joining them with a straight scarf. Glue the capping pieces in position, holding them with masking tape before winding heavy string tightly around them and wedging them down to ensure sufficient clamping pressure. Trim them when the glue is dry, using a spokeshave, or a router fitted with a trimming guide. Work a slight moulding or radius at the top edge with the simple tool illustrated.

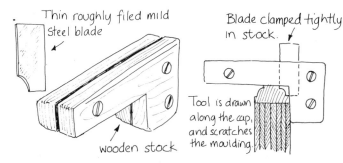

Thin roughly filed mild Steel blade

Blade clamped tightly in stock.

wooden stock

Tool is drawn along the cap, and scratches the moulding.

FOLDING SEATS

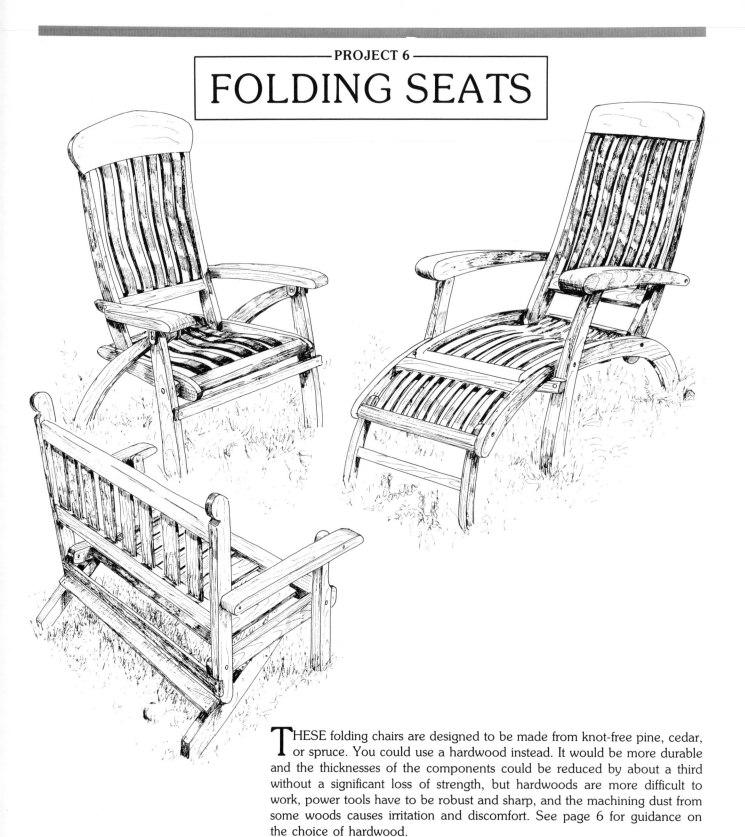

THESE folding chairs are designed to be made from knot-free pine, cedar, or spruce. You could use a hardwood instead. It would be more durable and the thicknesses of the components could be reduced by about a third without a significant loss of strength, but hardwoods are more difficult to work, power tools have to be robust and sharp, and the machining dust from some woods causes irritation and discomfort. See page 6 for guidance on the choice of hardwood.

Although these chairs may seem complicated, none of the mechanical processes involved in making them require much technical skill. Without a system of mass production, the work would be tedious, but not difficult. Here are a few suggestions for setting up your power tools to work on a production basis. By adopting some, and adapting and improving others, you will be exploring a new and absorbing aspect of woodwork, and using the machine tools in a manner in which they excel.

FOLDING SEAT-STEAMER

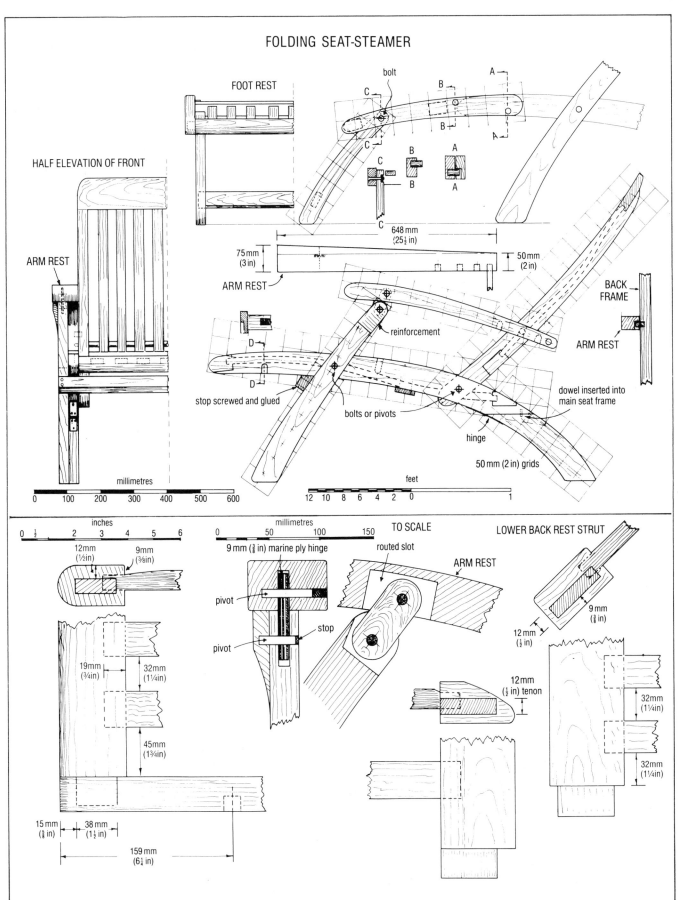

FOOT REST

bolt

HALF ELEVATION OF FRONT

ARM REST

648 mm
(25½ in)

75 mm
(3 in)

50 mm
(2 in)

ARM REST

BACK FRAME

ARM REST

reinforcement

stop screwed and glued

bolts or pivots

dowel inserted into main seat frame

hinge

50 mm (2 in) grids

millimetres

0   100   200   300   400   500   600

feet

12 10 8 6 4 2 0   1

inches

0 ½ 2 3 4 5 6

12mm
(½in)

9mm
(⅜in)

19mm
(¾in)

32mm
(1¼in)

45mm
(1¾in)

15 mm
(⅝in)

38 mm
(1½in)

159 mm
(6¼in)

millimetres

0   50   100   150

9 mm (⅜ in) marine ply hinge

pivot

pivot

stop

TO SCALE

routed slot

ARM REST

12mm
(½ in) tenon

LOWER BACK REST STRUT

9 mm
(⅜ in)

12 mm
(½ in)

32mm
(1¼in)

32mm
(1¼in)

FOLDING SEAT – PLANTER'S

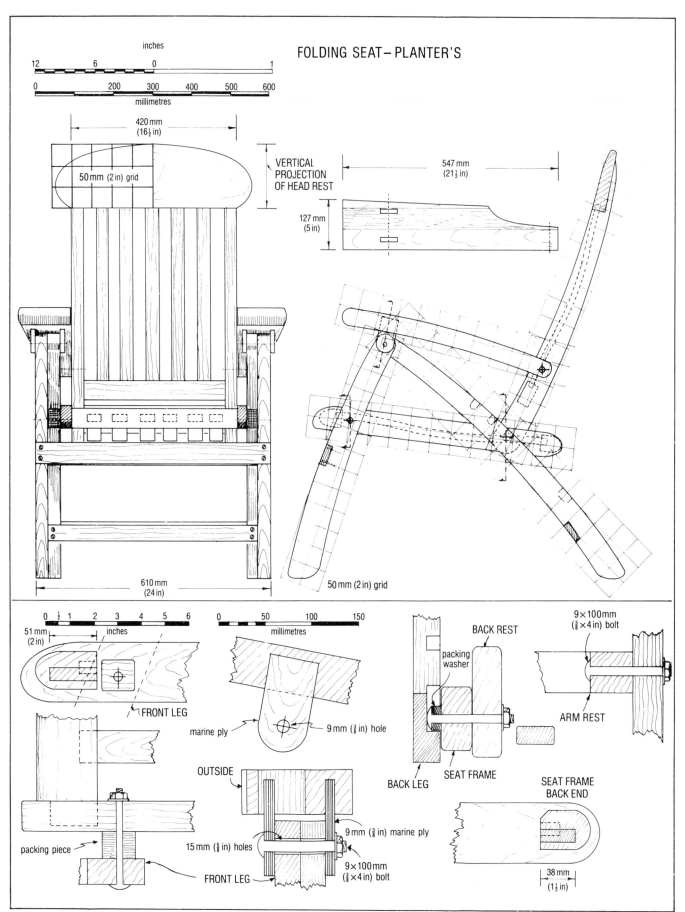

inches
12   6   0   1

0   200   300   400   500   600
millimetres

420 mm
(16½ in)

50 mm (2 in) grid

VERTICAL
PROJECTION
OF HEAD REST

547 mm
(21½ in)

127 mm
(5 in)

610 mm
(24 in)

50 mm (2 in) grid

0 ½ 1   2   3   4   5   6
inches

51 mm
(2 in)

FRONT LEG

0   50   100   150
millimetres

marine ply   9 mm (⅜ in) hole

packing piece

OUTSIDE

9 mm (⅜ in) marine ply

15 mm (⅝ in) holes

9×100 mm
(⅜×4 in) bolt

FRONT LEG

BACK REST

packing
washer

BACK LEG

SEAT FRAME

9×100 mm
(⅜×4 in) bolt

ARM REST

SEAT FRAME
BACK END

38 mm
(1½ in)

FOLDING BENCH

Cutting list
C 22×75 mm (1×3 in)
E 50×75 mm (2×3 in)

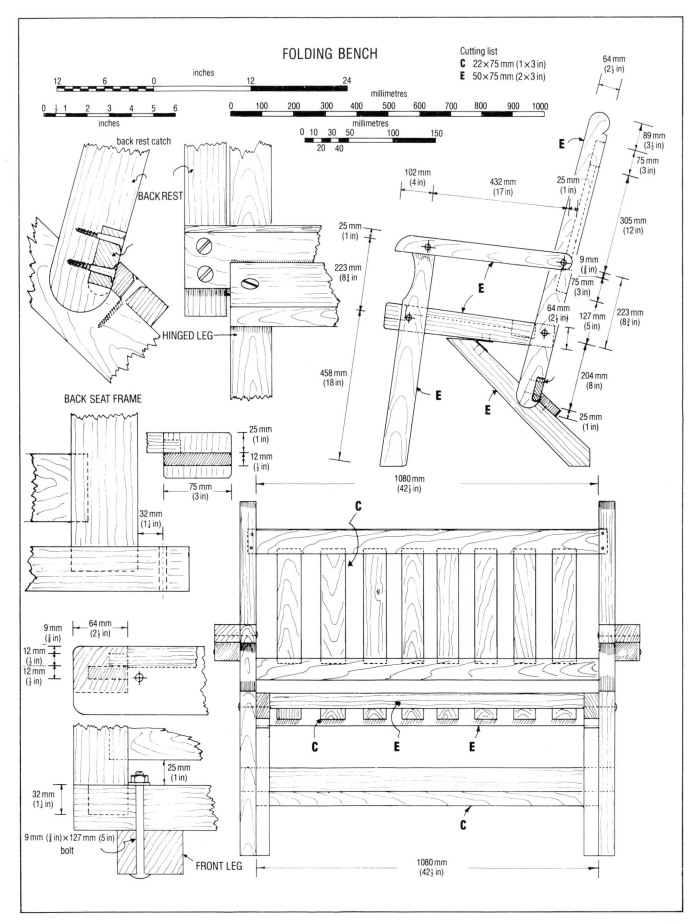

back rest catch

BACK REST

HINGED LEG

BACK SEAT FRAME

64 mm (2½ in)

89 mm (3½ in)

75 mm (3 in)

102 mm (4 in)

432 mm (17 in)

25 mm (1 in)

305 mm (12 in)

25 mm (1 in)

223 mm (8¾ in)

9 mm (⅜ in)

75 mm (3 in)

64 mm (2½ in)

127 mm (5 in)

223 mm (8¾ in)

204 mm (8 in)

25 mm (1 in)

458 mm (18 in)

1080 mm (42½ in)

25 mm (1 in)

12 mm (½ in)

75 mm (3 in)

32 mm (1¼ in)

9 mm (⅜ in)

64 mm (2½ in)

12 mm (½ in)

12 mm (½ in)

25 mm (1 in)

32 mm (1¼ in)

9 mm (⅜ in) × 127 mm (5 in) bolt

FRONT LEG

1080 mm (42½ in)

inches
millimetres
millimetres
inches

It is helpful to have the following tools: circular saw, jigsaw, router, belt sander and drill. Recommended accessories include the saw bench for mounting the circular saw, router bench for vertical milling, copy routing and drilling, and two special clamps to mount the belt sander on the workbench.

There is a strange discontinuity in preparing for a production run. Your preoccupation is with dimensions, jigs and templates. Making and adjusting them takes time, and a lot of thought and after a week of hard work, the end product seems no closer. Actually, when the planning and setting up is complete and tested, the work is all but done.

Working Sequence

■ First Stage

Draw a full-sized end elevation on a board. Make full-sized templates for each component, where necessary.

■ Second Stage

Saw the blanks, cut several spares of each component, stack them in groups. Drill and rebate them where necessary. Saw them roughly to shape, and machine them. Sand, smooth and round them, where necessary.

■ Third Stage

Cut the remaining joints, rebates, holes, etc. Fit the components together, with pivots, hinges, etc. Finish with stain or paint.

Draw out a full-size side elevation of the seat. Check the pivotting and folding operations, and adjust the positions of the pivots, the lengths and the curves where necessary to ensure that your full-sized version of these very small plans works.

First Stage

■ Templates

To ensure accuracy, you must have templates to control every element in the construction of the chair: shapes, joints, and fastenings. The purpose of a template is to guide a machine tool to make an accurate reproduction. Some templates can incorporate all the required features; in others, for example, where the position and distance between two holes are the only critical factors, the template can be basic. Make your templates from 4 mm ($^3/_{16}$ in) good quality plywood, or M.D.F. (Medium Density Fibreboard). Trace round the shapes of the different pieces, spray-mount the tracing on your template material, and cut it out. Finish your templates with files, sandpaper, and filler, where necessary to fair the curves and remove roughness at the edges. Check your work against the full-sized plans.

À number of methods for holding a template against a blank are described on page 58. They vary according to the conditions in which the template is being used. Sometimes it is necessary to screw the template to the blank and fill the screw holes afterwards. Under no circumstances use a template in a situation where its shape is altered by the machining process. For example, a simple stick template, locating the position of two holes, cannot be used as a drill guide because, in a repetitive process, the holes will enlarge.

Second Stage

■ Cutting Components to Length

Fit a depth stop on the right-angle guide on the saw bench, extending the arm of the guide to accommodate longer pieces plus the end stop, if necessary. For short lengths, arrange a stop on the saw table, and feed the stock across the right-angle guide. Do not use the parallel fence as the depth stop, because the pieces which you want will be flung into the saw blade as they are sawn off.

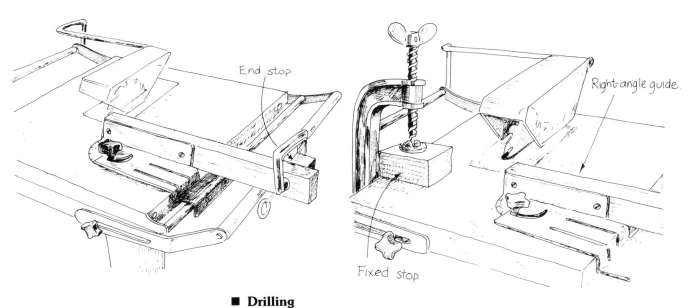

End stop

Right-angle guide.

Fixed stop

■ Drilling

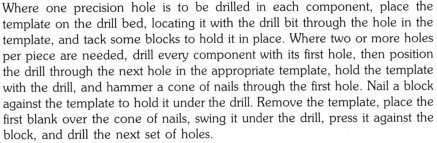

Drill held in pillar drill.

Where one precision hole is to be drilled in each component, place the template on the drill bed, locating it with the drill bit through the hole in the template, and tack some blocks to hold it in place. Where two or more holes per piece are needed, drill every component with its first hole, then position the drill through the next hole in the appropriate template, hold the template with the drill, and hammer a cone of nails through the first hole. Nail a block against the template to hold it under the drill. Remove the template, place the first blank over the cone of nails, swing it under the drill, press it against the block, and drill the next set of holes.

Every pivot hole should be drilled slightly oversize. When the wood swells the holes contract. You will need a 9 mm ($\frac{3}{8}$ in) or 10 mm ($\frac{7}{16}$ in) hole for an 8 mm ($\frac{5}{16}$ in) pivot rod.

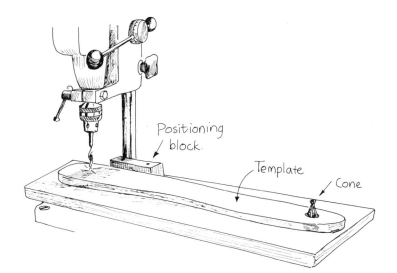

Positioning block.

Template

Cone

■ Rebating

If possible, work the rebates in the end of the board before cutting the board into blanks (i.e. before cutting out seat slats). Where you have to rebate narrow pieces, use a routing board, tacking one or two blocks on it to hold the wood in position. The advantage of using the board is that the router bears against a greater level surface. If the board is marked with all the angles you will need, you will be able to rout accurate shoulders without worrying too much about the angle and accuracy of the ends of the wood. If you have a router bench, cut rebates by raising and locking the height adjustment and working against the appropriate part of the shape template.

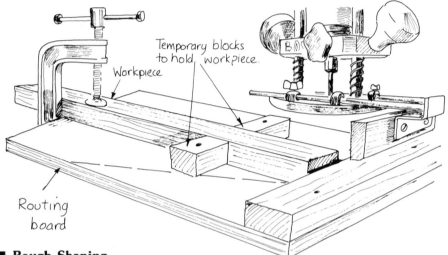

Temporary blocks to hold workpiece.

Workpiece

Routing board

■ Rough Shaping

Trim the blanks as accurately as you can with a jigsaw, leaving the last 1.5 mm (1/16 in) to be removed by router as described below. The difficulty in cutting out shapes from already thin blanks is that the more you trim away, the less level surface is left to steady the jigsaw. The trick is to cut round the line, but not to cut off the waste. Finish cuts just before they meet, and snap them off when you have finished sawing.

■ Accurate Shaping

Different methods of holding the blank to a shaping template are illustrated. The template holding the blank bears against a 6 mm (1/4 in) diameter pin set immediately beneath the 6 mm (1/4 in) two-flute router cutter. It will be seen that by using this system and utilising the plunge and depth stop facility of the router bench and stand, you can carry out internal routing with equal ease.

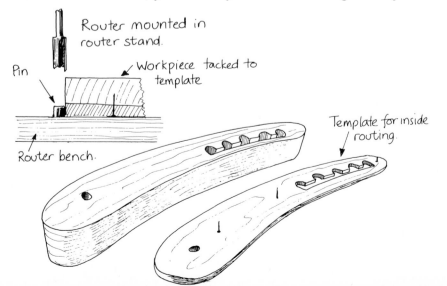

Router mounted in router stand.

Pin

Workpiece tacked to template

Router bench.

Template for inside routing.

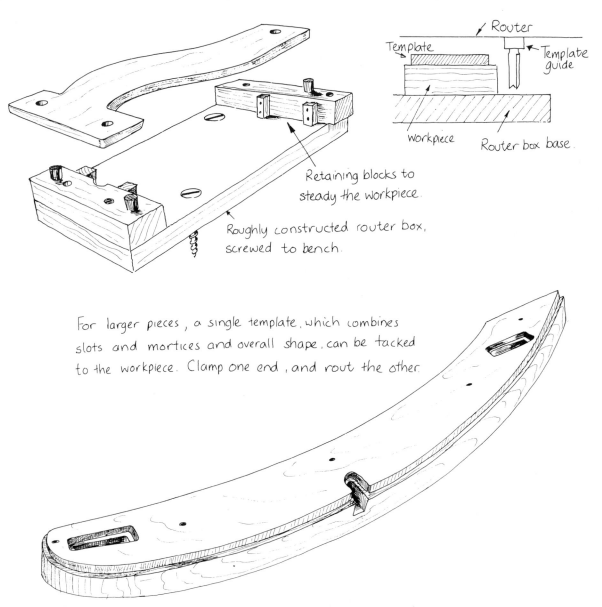

Template

Router

Template guide

workpiece

Router box base.

Retaining blocks to steady the workpiece.

Roughly constructed router box, screwed to bench.

For larger pieces, a single template, which combines slots and mortices and overall shape, can be tacked to the workpiece. Clamp one end, and rout the other.

Where the wood being shaped is thin and needs support, or where it is difficult or dangerous to grip the piece, a wide template is used, which only trims one side of the blank.

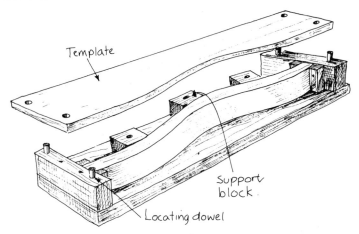

Template

Support block.

Locating dowel

If you do not have a router stand and bench, make a router box. This is a shallow tray with apertures in the sides, which is adapted to hold (by means of grooves, dowels, or screws), the roughly shaped blank. The blank is held down by a plywood board, which covers the tray and is located by four short dowels. This top board is the template, and its edge, or the slots cut in it, steer the router cutter. The profiles in the template are cut slightly undersize because the router bit is a narrower diameter than the guide. This is a good system where several separate templates can be used on the same blank.

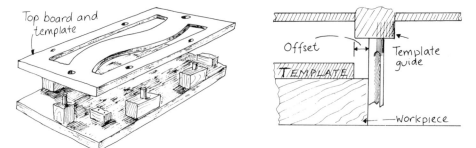

A variation of this is useful on such occasions as when the outside of the entire blank has to be shaped. The blank is screwed or bolted to the tray, and a slightly undersized template is tacked to the blank. The sides of the tray are at the same level as the top of the template, to give support. This is a useful and simple system, particularly on large pieces, where there are joints to plunge out, as well as all-round shaping.

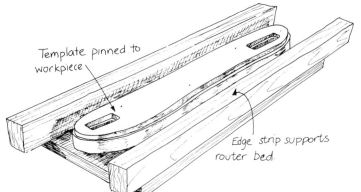

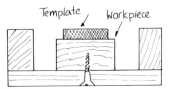

■ Sanding

Clamp the belt sander on its side, 4 mm (³⁄₁₆ in) above a sanding board. Tack a 4 mm (³⁄₁₆ in) fence immediately below the belt as illustrated, offset the fence, if you are using the routing template. With the template and the blank tacked together, sand the blank to remove any roughness. To smooth and slightly round narrow flat surfaces 35 mm (1½ in) or less fit a drum sander to the chuck of the electric drill, and shape them against the sanding drum. Arrange a vacuum cleaner to collect the sanding dust, and wear a face mask.

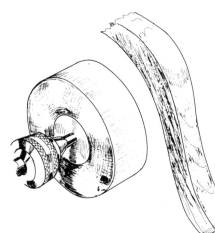

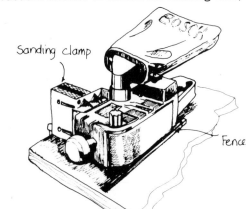

Third Stage

■ Tenoning

Angled tenons are best cut individually by handsaw, but all the straight tenons can be cut on the circular saw. Make up the tenon support jig and use as illustrated. Tenon depth is altered by adjusting the rise and fall of the circular saw blade. Shoulders are set from a line pencilled or scribed on the saw table. Tenons with sloping shoulders can be cut by holding the blank at an angle, and tacking on a support batten.

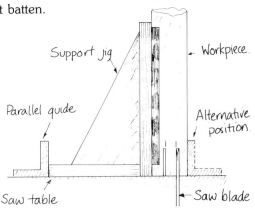

Support jig

Workpiece.

Parallel guide

Alternative position.

Saw table

Saw blade

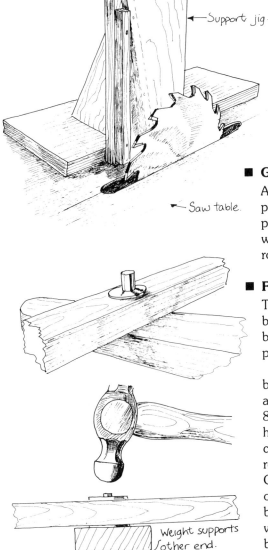

Support jig.

Saw table.

■ Glueing Up

Accuracy is essential. Impose complete dimensional control by glueing up the parts on a flat board, tacking retaining blocks around a full-size outline of the piece you are assembling. It is then an easy matter to arrange more blocks, wedges and tourniquets to pull the joints together. Insert the pivot rods and rotate them to check the holes are aligned.

■ Fastening

The pivot rods in the chairs illustrated are made from steel rod. Bronze would be ideal and brass is satisfactory but, like steel, it will corrode. Most blacksmiths and light engineering works will sell 8 mm (5/16 in) steel rod, precision engineering suppliers will have brass and bronze rod.

Assembling the chairs now involves inserting the rods, slipping washers between components to stop them rubbing each other, rivetting the pivots, and screwing on the hinges. For rivetting each rod, you need one close fitting 8 mm (5/16 in) washer at each end, and a ball pein hammer, a hacksaw and a heavy block of iron, or large vice. Push the rod right through the interlocking components of the hinge, and slip a washer over the far end. Then tap the rod back, until only 1.5 mm (1/16 in) of the rod protrudes beyond the washer. Cut off the spare rod, leaving 3 mm (1/8 in) proud, and slip the other washer over it. Now hold the chair on its side, rest one end of the rod on the metal block, and tap the other end at the edge of the rod until a slight burr stops the washer from falling off. Turn the chair over and repeat at the other end, beating the end of the rod into a shallow dome. Finish the dome on the first side, and the job is done.

Weight supports other end.

Rod end hammered into a dome.

■ Hinges

Use galvanised, stainless steel or bronze hinges, which are obtainable from ironmongers or boat chandlers. Fasten the hinges with countersunk screws of the same material as the hinges. To prevent the hinges from loosening as a result of shear forces, drive a screw which is much longer than the others into each flap of the hinge, letting it poke out of the other side of the wood. Rivet a washer over its point.

Position the hinges as on the plans. They do not need to be recessed. If you are unsure of the exact position for the hinge, fit it with one or two short screws, and replace them with longer ones when you find the correct position.

GLUEING

Garden furniture is built to be neglected. These classic pieces are designed to survive intermittent maintenance or neglect. They are solid, and fitted together with concealed joints. There are few bolts, screws or nails to react with the wood or allow the ingress of moisture. If the joints hold up, these pieces of furniture will last for as long as the wood itself retains its integrity and strength.

Dry wood is much stronger than wet wood, and lasts almost indefinitely. If a finish forms a perfect seal encasing the wood, and the seal adheres in all conditions and weathers, the piece of furniture will have total protection from the weather. The only finish which provides this protection is one which seals the wood in a clear, essentially impermeable coating of epoxy resin, to protect from damp and wet conditions. This is the ultimate finish for garden furniture made from non-durable woods, but it is expensive.

Glue Type	Trade Name	Moisture Content of Wood	Weather-proof	Gap Filling	Notes
Epoxy resin with fillers	Resin 105 Hardener 206 (slow) 5:1 weight	8–12%	Weather-proof	With 406 Coloidal Silica added, up to 6 mm (¼ in) without strength loss.	Three coats unfilled provides weather-proof protective coating. With thickeners added, this is a powerful gap-filling glue. Add thickeners and hardeners to ready mixed resin, then pour into an open tray to reduce temperature of exothermic reaction. High temperatures in the glue pot cut the pot life of mixed glue.
Epoxy resin	Thixotropic 1:1 volume	8–12%	Weather-proof	Up to 6 mm (¼ in) without strength loss.	Durable and transparent glue. A glue-join stronger than wood. Clean hands with resin removing cream, wear barrier cream or gloves. Clean tools with West cleaning solvent.
Resorcinol resin	Cascophen RS-216, Catalyst RXS-8 5:1 weight	18% max	Weather-proof	Gap filling up to about 1.5mm (¹⁄₁₆ in) without strength loss. Bigger cavities filled, provided glue does not run out.	An alternative to epoxy. Dries to deep red colour, so unsuited for most varnished or stained work. Clean away excess glue with water. Wear gloves or barrier cream. Catalyst can cause dermatitis.
Urea-formaldehyde	Cascamite (add water)	18% max	Water-proof	Hardens in cavities, but strength loss.	Almost transparent, can be used under an impermeable paint or varnish finish. Wipe off excess with damp rag before it sets.
P.V.A.	Woodworker's exterior white glue	18%	Water-proof	Not gap filling.	Only suitable where joints are good, and sealed by impermeable weatherproof coat. Non-mechanical joints (i.e. scarfs) liable to creep under load.

For availability of glues, see the addresses in the Appendix.

Two finishes are recommended for garden furniture made from non-durable woods – the West System Epoxy, or a microporous long-lasting paint or stain which allows timber to breathe, thereby preventing decay. Resorcinol and epoxy resin glues are the only glues that should be used to hold the furniture together. This furniture has been designed to be glued together with either resorcinol or epoxy resin glues, which are weatherproof. Waterproof glues (which conform to a less rigorous specification than weatherproof glues) such as P.V.A. or Urea-formaldehyde glues can be used instead, but the quality of the glue joints will be totally dependent upon proper and regular attention to a conventional high maintenance exterior finish.

The chart features some of the glues available.

■ Moisture Content

Wood obtained from a D.I.Y. store, and wood that is sold tightly wrapped in polythene will have a moisture content of less than 20%. If you are uncertain whether the wood is dry enough to glue, bring it into the house, and stack it in a warm dry place, out of the sun, for as long as possible, but at least two weeks.

■ Mixing Glue

All glue kits are supplied with full instructions. Note that with epoxy resin, the heat generated by mixing the resin and hardener (exothermic reaction) accelerates the hardening process. If you have a complex glueing project, divide it into parts so you are not driven by the speed with which your expensive glue is hardening. Mix small quantities at a time, or surround your glue pot with ice cubes held in a polythene bag to prolong its pot life.

■ Temperatures

The pot life of West System epoxy resin 105/206 at 21°C (70°F) is about 20–25 minutes in 100 gram mass. (Note: Other hardeners have different gelation times.) For resorcinol resin at the same temperatures it is about 3¾ hours. Curing time in a thin section at 21°C (70°F) is 9 hours and 7 hours respectively. Full strength is reached after about 5–7 days. Resorcinol glue is sensitive to air temperature, which should be above 15°C (60°F). Epoxy can be used in lower temperatures but hardening is delayed, and the uncured glue is vulnerable to atmospheric moisture.

■ Glueing Together

Ensure that you have enough glue, rubber gloves, mixing containers, and mixing sticks. If you are going to use thickened epoxy resin, mask off wood close to the joint to limit the spread of the sticky glue. Clear the work bench or table, and lay out sheets of newspaper to catch glue drops. Ensure you have plenty of suitable clamps, and wooden or cardboard pads to prevent the clamps marking the wood. Check that every joint pulls up, and that your scheme for fixing and clamping works.

Now, stop and check that you have enough time to glue together your project. Mix up sufficient adhesive for the job in hand, but if using epoxy, remember to mix only small batches of resin and hardener, thereby avoiding premature gelation because of the heat build-up. Apply glue to both surfaces and assemble.

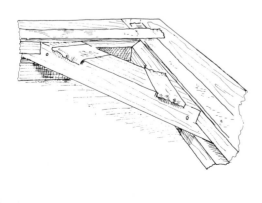

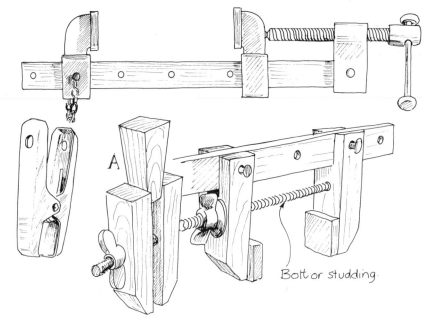

Bolt or studding.

■ Clamping

Do not apply clamping pressure immediately after assembly unless you are glueing a joint which has inherent mechanical strength (such as a mortice and tenon, or a cross-halving). The resin must be allowed to thoroughly wet-out the timber surfaces before clamping. When using epoxy resins, excessive clamping pressure will produce a glue-starved joint and care must be taken during this operation. Five clamping devices are illustrated.

Check the clamps have not pulled or distorted the work, then wipe off the excess glue with a rag or brush, and leave it to harden.

■ Cleaning Up

Clean off excess epoxy glue before it hardens. A wooden scraper or a rag moistened in solvent will easily remove drips and runs which will be difficult to sand or chisel away later. When using resorcinol resin, the excess adhesive can be wiped away with water. It is important to do this as unwanted resorcinol left on timber surfaces will stain the wood.

■ Reinforcing and Sealing

In some jobs where you are using epoxy resin, there is an opportunity to reinforce and seal a join by using excess glue as a fillet. The filleting compound is produced by adding one of the West System fillers (406 Colloidal Silica is a good, high strength material) to the mixed resin and hardener, until a paste-like consistency is achieved. Apply the filleting mixture along the joint line with a mixing stick and shape the fillet with a shaped tool, leaving a smooth, cove shape at the joint. Mask off the clean wood, then run left-over glue into the joint, and use a curved end of a flat stick to scrape and mould the glue into a radius. The filled epoxy resin handles very much like the silicone sealer used around bath tubs, and it will seal and strengthen the joint.

A VERY-WELL-EQUIPPED WORKSHOP

TWO GARDEN CHAIRS AND
THE DOUGLAS TABLE
(page 36 and page 72)

CONVERSATION CHAIR
(page 46)

GARDEN SEAT WITH CHINESE CHIPPENDALE DECORATIVE BACK
(page 16)

FOLDING SEAT
(page 52)

ORCHARD BENCH
(page 22)

SUN LOUNGER
(page 96)

TREE SEAT
(page 92)

BROOK HOUSE TABLE WITH ARMCHAIR
(page 76)

PLANTERS
(page 100)

CHAMPHERING

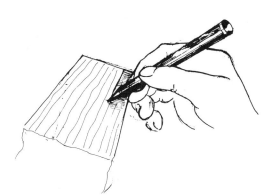

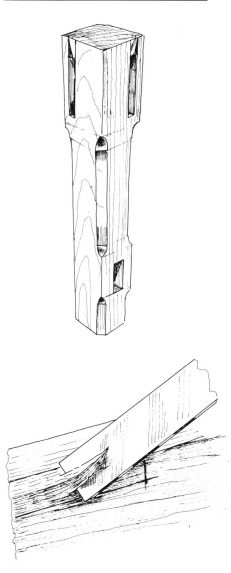

Champhering the corners of the legs makes the table look more elegant. Champhering starts above or below the joints. Do not run the champher over the joints. Mark the champhers by hand, but check with a set square that they start and finish at the same heights. Practise cutting a champher on some scrap wood before venturing onto the legs: it is not easy to do an accurate job but, luckily, provided the ends of the champhers are neat and in line, inaccuracies elsewhere do not matter very much.

Strop the 15 mm (⅝ in) chisel until it is really sharp, then, starting close to one end, cut down in a single sweep, level out, and cut along the line. If the blade is difficult to control, you are either trying to remove too much wood in one go, or you are working against the grain, and should turn the leg round. Shave down the corner until you are almost at the pencil marks. Rest the back of the chisel flat against the champher, and using the blade in a planing motion, slice away unevennesses. Stop the chisel as you reach the other end of the champher. Finish off the champher with a clean incision as illustrated. Repeat at the other end, and then make two sweeping cuts to finish.

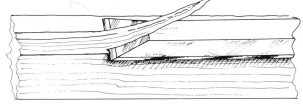

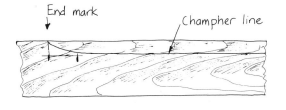

End mark

Champher line

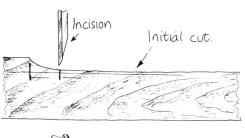

Incision

Initial cut.

Shaving action reveals end cut

Finishing cut.

LONG GARDEN TABLE

THIS garden table will seat six people. It is easy to build and economical in materials. The 'H' stretcher is optional. It gives additional strength, but those who like to have a clear space beneath the table for legs, bags, dogs and children can omit it.

No special clamps are required to pull together the joints of this long table while it is glueing. Pegged tenons draw up the joints and the method of marking and cutting them is described on page 29. The slatted top allows air to circulate beneath and around the planking, reducing the likelihood of rot. Note that the table frame is screwed to the top through the side rails, and that small rectangular packing pieces, aligned with the slats and glued to them, lift the top clear of the framework. Note also the decorative earpieces at the ends of the side rails, which are glued there prior to shaping, and tenoned into the legs to strengthen the joint. There are also instructions for champhering and making a hole for a parasol.

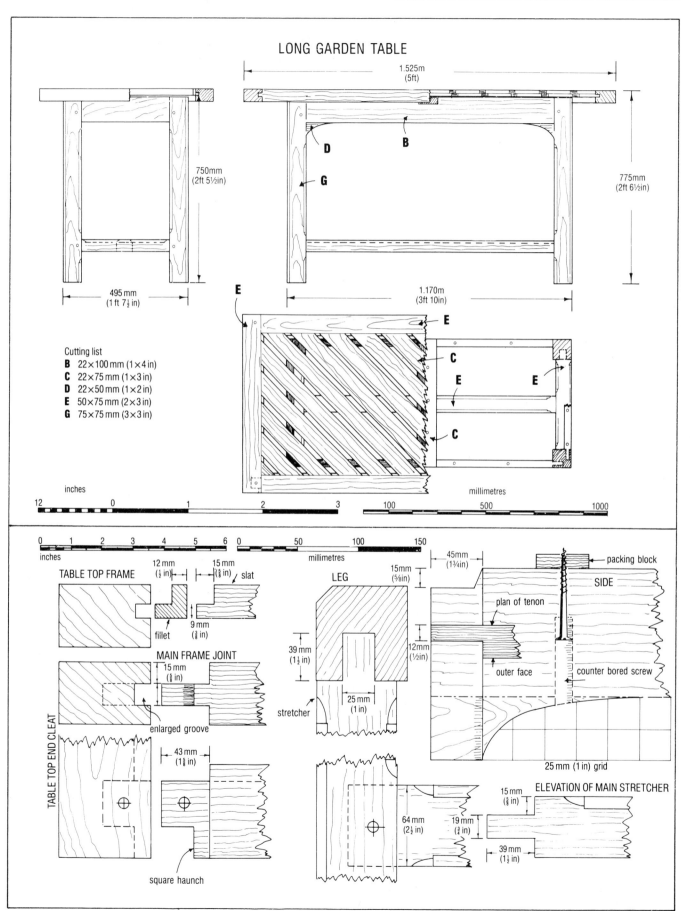

LONG GARDEN TABLE

1.525m
(5ft)

750mm
(2ft 5½in)

775mm
(2ft 6½in)

495 mm
(1 ft 7½ in)

1.170m
(3ft 10in)

B

D

G

B

E

E

C

E

E

C

C

Cutting list
B 22×100 mm (1×4 in)
C 22×75 mm (1×3 in)
D 22×50 mm (1×2 in)
E 50×75 mm (2×3 in)
G 75×75 mm (3×3 in)

inches

12   0   1   2   3

millimetres

100   500   1000

0 1 2 3 4 5 6
inches

0   50   100   150
millimetres

TABLE TOP FRAME

12 mm
(½ in)

15 mm
(⅝ in)

slat

fillet

9 mm
(⅜ in)

MAIN FRAME JOINT

15 mm
(⅝ in)

enlarged groove

TABLE TOP END CLEAT

43 mm
(1⅝ in)

square haunch

LEG

39 mm
(1½ in)

25 mm
(1 in)

stretcher

15 mm
(⅝ in)

12 mm
(½in)

64 mm
(2½ in)

19 mm
(¾ in)

45mm
(1¾in)

packing block

SIDE

plan of tenon

outer face

counter bored screw

25 mm (1 in) grid

ELEVATION OF MAIN STRETCHER

15 mm
(⅝ in)

39 mm
(1½ in)

Construction

■ Framework

The legs are cut to length and morticed first, and the end rails and stretchers are tenoned in. With the earpieces glued on, the side rails can be tenoned, and fitted into the legs. Shape the earpieces (see page 71) with a jigsaw or multi-purpose saw fitted with a fine blade, after the tenons have been trimmed. Now fit the main stretcher which is, as you can see from the plans, slightly longer than the side rails. Pencil in the champhering lines, and champher the legs.

■ Assembling the Framework

Glue and peg the ends first. Then invert the legs and rails, and glue on the sides. Assemble the framework while it is upside down, because if the joints fall apart before the pegs are driven in, the mortices are less likely to be damaged. Fit the main stretcher last. When the glue has hardened, turn the table framework up the right way, and cut out and sink the cross brace into the side rails. This is marked and cut like a cross-halving joint, finishing with the brace flush with the rails.

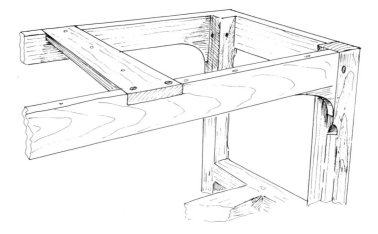

■ Top

Cut out the top framework. Mark the mortice and tenon joints clearly, then rout the groove round the inside edge of the four framework pieces. Check the mortice and tenon marks, and adjust them if you find the groove you have just cut has reduced the width of the tenons. Rout out the mortices and saw the tenons in the sides. Assemble the joints and drill them for pegging.

Lay the tabletop framework on a flat board and nail blocks round three sides to hold it. Glue the joints at one end and drive in the pegs. Remove the other end. Now make up a filler strip that slips neatly into the framework groove, adjust the circular saw angle guide to cut at 45°, and saw it into 25 mm (1 in) lengths.

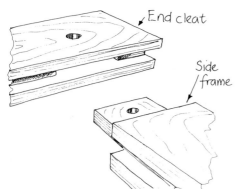

End cleat

Side frame

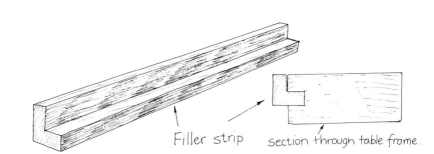

Filler strip   Section through table frame.

■ Diagonal Slats

Every slat has two rebates which slot into the table framework and hold it in position.

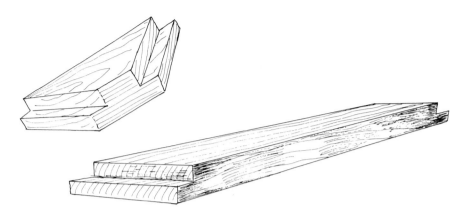

Fit the short end slats first, using the routing board illustrated to give stability and guidance to the router when it is cutting the rebates. Slip two 25 mm (1 in) offcuts between the slats to space them accurately. Follow with the longer slats. These are all identical. These can be cut three at a time from a wide plank, and cut into strips with the circular saw afterwards, to save time. When one end and all the longer slats are fitted, close off the second end cleat, peg it and fit the remaining slats, working towards the centre of the tabletop. Fit the slats using plenty of glue. Glue and press a filler piece into each groove after every slat has been fitted.

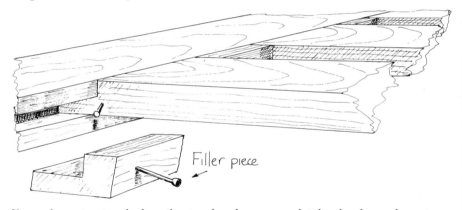

Filler piece

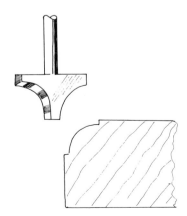

If you have to stop before the top has been completely glued up, do not worry. Wipe the glue out of the groove and hold your last slat with two filler pieces pinned in place with stainless steel panel pins. While the glue is still workable, pin other, less well-fitting filler pieces. If you have some surplus glue, press a mixture of glue and sanding dust into any remaining cavities and clean with a flat knife. Later, you can continue to build up the tabletop. Remove or loosen the end frame to facilitate trimming the last few slats. When they are all fitting, glue up the end joints, and fit the last few slats and filler pieces. When the glue is dry, clean up the top with a belt sander. Use an orbital sander to remove sharp edges, and to complete the smoothing. Round the outside corners of the table, and rout a fine thumbnail moulding around the top edge with a router and following wheel.

■ Fitting the Top of the Base

Make a hole for a parasol (see page 71), if required. Sand the framework with the orbital sander, but leave the corners, champhers, etc. well defined. Now fit and glue the packing pieces beneath the top and drill the rails as illustrated for screwing on the top. If you are planning to paint the table, paint the underside and the top of the rails and legs with a generous coat of microporous paint. Squirt silicone bathroom sealer into the screwholes in the top of the rails, before lowering the top into place and screwing it tight. Finish painting the table.

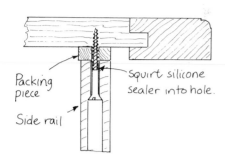

Packing piece

Side rail

Squirt silicone sealer into hole.

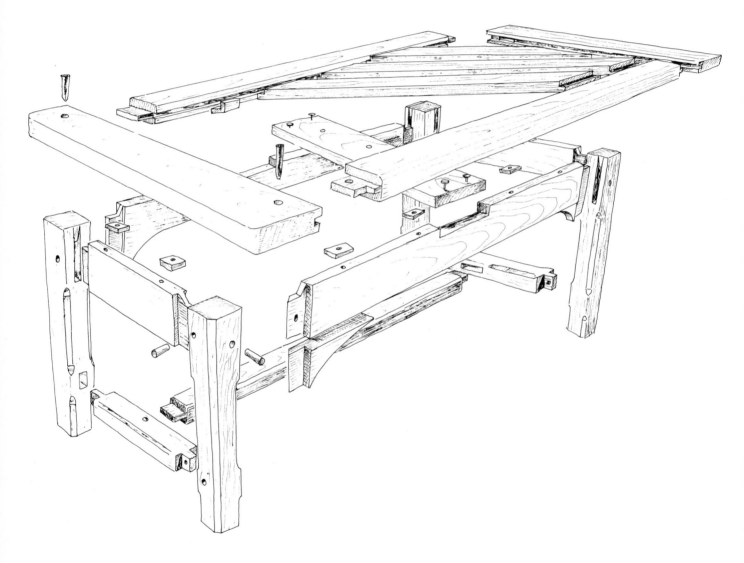

EARPIECES

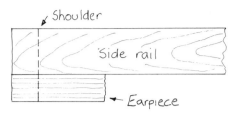

The grain of the earpiece should run parallel to the rail. Glue the earpieces to the rail, holding each one in place with a clamp, or string and wedges. Plane up the outer surfaces when the glue is dry, and mark in the tenons. Cut the tenons with a router, or hand saw, before shaping the earpiece. Take the shape of the earpiece from the drawings, or design your own, but avoid delicate curves that expose vulnerable short-grain wood, because one day they will break off.

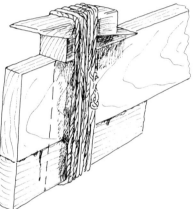

PARASOL HOLE

Mark in the position and diameter of the pole on the centre cross brace, and drill it with a tank cutter, drilling from the opposite side when the cutter is half-way through. Lift the top, place it in position and mark off the hole. Glue reinforcement pieces between the slats on the top, extending them 100 mm (4 in) beyond the centre of the hole. Hold them tightly with tapered wedges until the glue is cured, then drill out the hole, starting from the other side when you reach midway. Finish the table top, and drill a shallow recess in the stretcher to receive the point of the pole. Drill an additional hole to drain the recess.

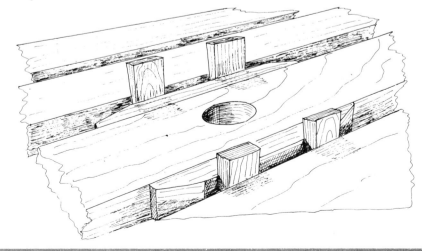

DOUGLAS TABLE

THIS is an attractive and convenient garden table. It is strong enough to sit on and high enough to use for a casual tea party. The mitred and slatted top is screwed and glued directly onto the side rails, which are reinforced at the corners with earpieces. The corners of the legs and top framework are rounded after assembly, either with a plain radius, or with a fine thumbnail moulding using a quadrant router cutter.

THE DOUGLAS TABLE

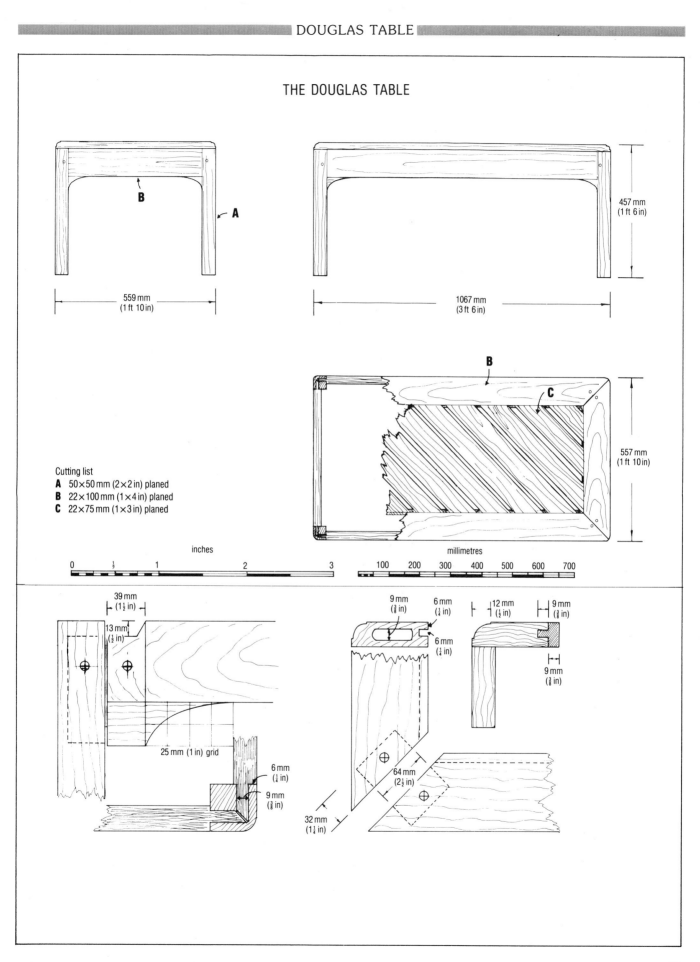

Cutting list

A 50×50 mm (2×2 in) planed
B 22×100 mm (1×4 in) planed
C 22×75 mm (1×3 in) planed

559 mm
(1 ft 10 in)

457 mm
(1 ft 6 in)

1067 mm
(3 ft 6 in)

557 mm
(1 ft 10 in)

inches

0   ½   1   2   3

millimetres

100 200 300 400 500 600 700

39 mm
(1½ in)

13 mm
(½ in)

25 mm (1 in) grid

6 mm
(¼ in)

9 mm
(⅜ in)

9 mm
(⅜ in)

6 mm
(¼ in)

6 mm
(¼ in)

12 mm
(½ in)

9 mm
(⅜ in)

9 mm
(⅜ in)

64 mm
(2½ in)

32 mm
(1¼ in)

Construction

■ Base Framework

Cut the side rails to length, (include the tenons in the overall measurements) and glue on the earpiece blanks at the end of each rail, holding them with clamps, string and wedges. Plane up the surface of the rails when the glue has cured, and cut the tenons at the ends. Saw the outline of the earpiece, using a jigsaw or multi-purpose saw fitted with a fine blade. Sand the outer face smooth.

Cut the legs to length, and mortice them with a router and an 8 mm (³⁄₈ in) cutter, stopping the mortice 12 mm (½ in) from the top of the leg. Trim the tenons, then peg and glue each mortice, testing the diagonals of the framework for squareness, and sighting the rails for level, before leaving the glue to harden.

■ Top

Cut the lengths for the top framework. Mark the face-side and face edge, and groove the face edge with the 6 mm (¼ in) router cutter. Mark off the mitre joints, either with a sliding bevel set to 45°, or by squaring off the ends of each plank and marking in the diagonal. Cut the mitres with a tenon saw, and trim them with a small block plane, until they are square with the face side, and all four joints fit together to form a neat mitred frame.

Number off the adjacent faces. Make up four loose tenons from 9 mm (³⁄₈ in) exterior ply, or hardwood offcuts. The tenons should be rectangular, identical in size and, when placed in position, should overlap each side by 32 mm (1¼ in), which is about as far as you can plunge the router. Mark off on the face-side of each joint the position of the tenon, placing it as far into the corner as possible, without it breaking out at the edge. Set up the router box and rout out four of the joints. Rearrange the router box, so that the face-side of the planks are still hard against the same side of the box. Keeping the fence adjustment, rout out the remaining four joints.

■ Fitting the Slats

Make up a 1 metre (3 foot) length of filler piece and cut the filler blocks to length on the circular saw, setting the adjustable guide to 45°, and setting a stop on the saw table to ensure that they are all the same length, (see page 57). Now peg the tenons in position (see page 29) but do not glue the joints. Just lay the top frame onto the legs and cut and fit the table top slats. The middle slats will be a standard length and shape, and can be rebated and sawn as a group, but at the ends they will all be different, and have to be fitted individually. Cut them to length, and lay them in position on the table framework, separated by a filler piece at each end. As each slat is placed in position on the framework, mark on its underside the shoulder line for the rebate. Number off the slats so you know where they fit in the frame and then, using the routing board, rout the rebate on their undersides. Replace

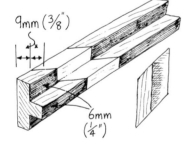

9mm (³⁄₈")

6mm (¼")

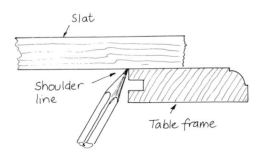

Slat

Shoulder line

Table frame

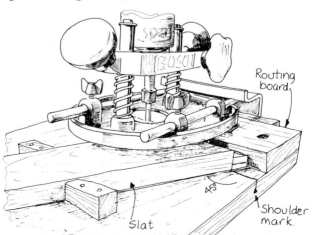

Routing board.

45°

Slat

Shoulder mark.

them; each one should drop tightly into the top framework. When you know the slat shoulders are correct, and you have noted and changed the marks for those that are not quite so good, square round the slats, and rout the upper rebate to complete the tongue. Check that at each end the slat fits neatly into a sample length of groove. When you have all the pieces ready, place the table top frame on a flat board covered with newspaper. Nail blocks around three sides to hold it in shape, glue and peg two end framework joints, and brush glue into the grooves.

Slide in the slats and filler pieces, brushing glue onto the tongues as they are fitted. When the last long diagonal is fitted, glue and peg up the other end, and fit the remaining slats, working from the corner towards the long diagonal, pressing in the filler pieces as you go. Tack any loosely fitting filler pieces with stainless steel panel pins. Leave the tabletop surrounded by the holding blocks, pressed on the flat board until the glue is dry.

■ Assembly

Sand the underside and screw and glue the top to the table framework. Fill and sand any remaining cavities, and rout the thumbnail moulding around the edges of the top. Round the corners of the legs and prepare for painting.

BROOK HOUSE TABLE

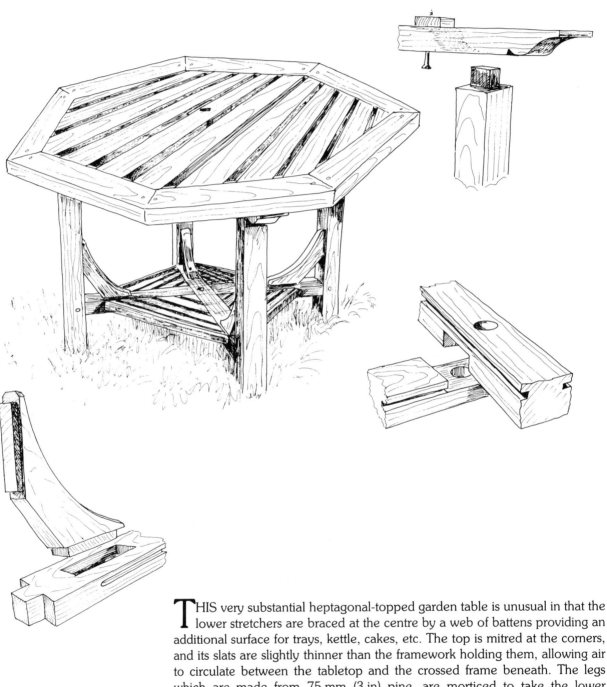

THIS very substantial heptagonal-topped garden table is unusual in that the lower stretchers are braced at the centre by a web of battens providing an additional surface for trays, kettle, cakes, etc. The top is mitred at the corners, and its slats are slightly thinner than the framework holding them, allowing air to circulate between the tabletop and the crossed frame beneath. The legs which are made from 75 mm (3 in) pine, are morticed to take the lower stretcher, grooved just above the mortice to receive the diagonal strut, and have a stub tenon sawn in their tops to hold the table top supports. Both the lower and the upper horizontal framework connecting the legs cross at the centre of the table, with a simple cross-halving joint. The lower one is strengthened by the web of battens which form the additional surface at the lower tier.

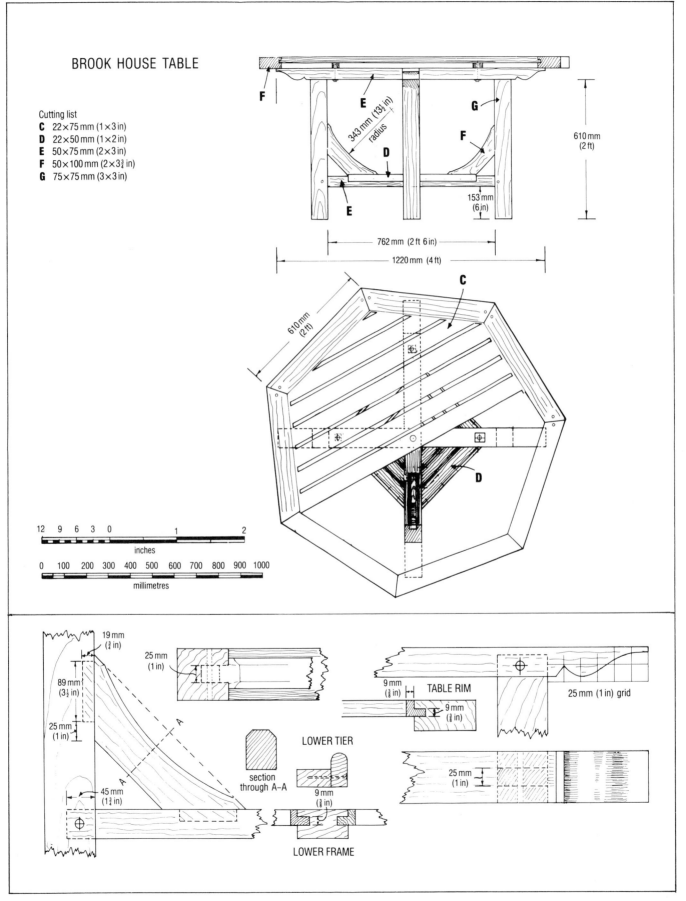

BROOK HOUSE TABLE

Cutting list
C 22×75 mm (1×3 in)
D 22×50 mm (1×2 in)
E 50×75 mm (2×3 in)
F 50×100 mm (2×3¾ in)
G 75×75 mm (3×3 in)

343 mm (13½ in) radius

610 mm (2 ft)

153 mm (6 in)

762 mm (2 ft 6 in)

1220 mm (4 ft)

610 mm (2 ft)

12 9 6 3 0   1   2
inches

0 100 200 300 400 500 600 700 800 900 1000
millimetres

19 mm (¾ in)

89 mm (3½ in)

25 mm (1 in)

45 mm (1¾ in)

25 mm (1 in)

section through A–A

LOWER TIER

9 mm (⅜ in)

LOWER FRAME

9 mm (⅜ in)

TABLE RIM

9 mm (⅜ in)

25 mm (1 in) grid

25 mm (1 in)

Construction

■ Base Framework

Cut the legs to length first, and remember to include the stub tenon at the top of each leg. Mark off and rout the mortices on the lower inside face of each leg, and rout the 50 mm (2 in) slots for the diagonal struts above. Saw the stub tenon, making the downward saw cuts first, then saw off the shoulders with a tenon saw. Rely on a chisel to trim the shoulder, ensuring that the surface is square and clean. Cut the cross-members to length. Mark off and cut the tenons at the ends of the lower cross, and mark the position for the halving joint. Check very carefully that the marking out of this joint is accurate. The cross halving is difficult to do well. The trick is to mark the exact widths of the pieces with a very sharp knife, and then, after squaring up the marks, cut right to the inside of the lines. This should make the joint a very tight press fit, which is what you want, since it may have to be taken apart a few times before it is glued up.

Mark in and rout out the 8 mm (³⁄₈ in) deep grooves for the lower tier and the groove for the diagonal strut, and saw and fit the tenons into the leg mortices. Cut and fit the diagonal struts in position, then glue the legs and diagonal struts together, drawing up the tenons with tapered pegs, as described on page 29. Check the legs are parallel and at right angles to the cross-piece, and tack battens across them to correct them if they are not, then leave the glue to cure.

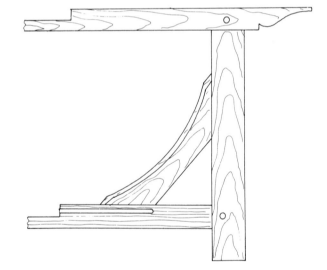

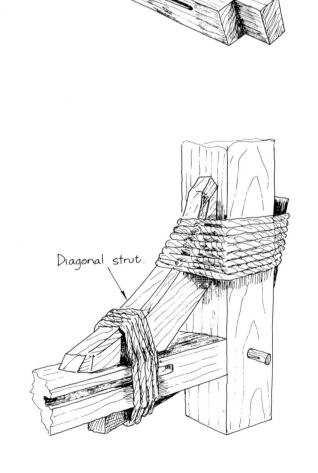

Diagonal strut.

■ Assembling the Base

Now glue and clamp up the main lower cross halving joint, and when the glue is dry, fit the lower tier of thin battens. The lower tier is made from narrow battens in exactly the same way that the top is made, except that at the outer edge there is a small lip moulding glued and pinned to the last batten, which closes off the groove. Fit the first batten in the apex of the triangle formed by the cross-halved joint, holding it in place with glue and a stainless steel panel pin. Use narrow filler pieces between the battens to block the groove and hold the battens in place. The gaps between the battens should not be more than 9 mm (3⁄8 in), or less than 6 mm (1⁄4 mm). Air should circulate between them, but not spoons!

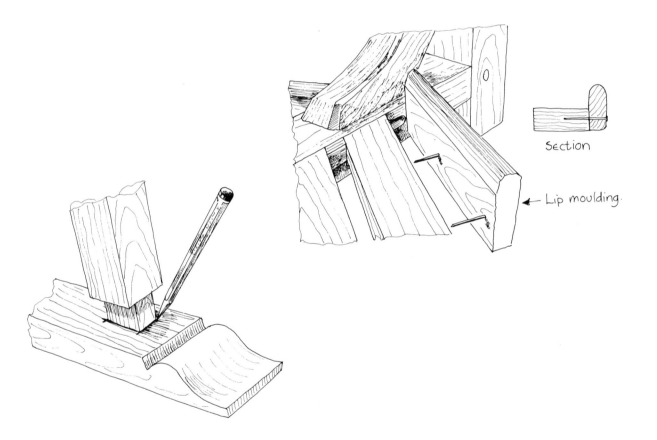

Section

← Lip moulding.

The upper cross halving is more difficult to make because the boards being joined are wider than those below. It is easier to chisel out the wide waste if the wood is weakened by additional sawcuts down to the half-way line. As with nearly all chiselling, use the tool in the direction where the grain lifts the cutting edge out of the wood. This enables the joint to be cut quickly, with little danger of the point of the chisel emerging below the marking line on the far side. Turn the wood round for the final shavings that level the joint. Now cut the profiled ends in the top cross-pieces, as described on page 44.

Glue and clamp the top cross halving joint, and then mark off the position of the mortices in the ends. The dimensions for these can be taken straight from the framework, if you lower the inverted legs and position them over the underside of the cross-halved frame. Square up your lines, and drill out the centres of the mortices, stopping the hole before boring right through the wood. Chop out the mortices to their finished size with a 15 mm (5⁄8 in) chisel. Glue the top framework in position so that the base is complete.

■ **Top**

The top is made in the same way as that on page 68 except that the corners of the upper framework are mitred. As you can see in the plans, the slats making up the surface of the table are narrower than the side framework, leaving an air gap between the crossed top framework and the top, which will only be bridged where packing pieces are inserted when the top is screwed down.

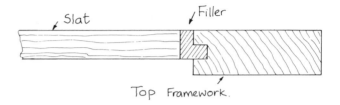

■ **Assembling the Top**

Make up the tabletop on a strong flat board. Mark and fit the slats individually, positioning them beneath the frame when marking out their shoulders. Rebate the ends of the slats, clamping them to the routing board. Several of the angles will be the same, and it will be worthwhile pencilling in the angles on the base of the router board, so you can reproduce the angles easily.

■ **Assembling the Table**

Peg and glue together three framework joints and rest the main part on a flat board, with wood blocks round it to hold it in position. Glue and peg together the remaining two parts of the top framework and loosely position it in place on the board. Fit and glue the slats, slipping filler pieces between the slats as you build up the top. When the long centre slats are in position, glue together the framework, and fit the last few slats, working from the outside towards the centre. Check all the filler pieces, and hold them with a stainless steel panel pin if they seem loose, then add sanding dust to the glue and fill remaining crevices.

Drill the parasol hole in the centre slat, and also a hole through the centre of the upper cross halved framework member, and then apply preservative to the table. Stain or paint the underside of the table and the top of the frame. Then assemble the table, using four coach screws with washers, which you should grease before screwing down the top as illustrated. Sand the top and edges.

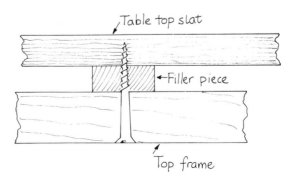

■ Shaping the Ends of the Top Frame

The simple curve at the end of the top cross-members cannot be sawn out with the jigsaw, because the plank is too wide. Draw the profile for the ends on some card, and cut it out to make a template. Transfer the shape onto the ends of the top cross-frame, marking on both sides and squaring across with a set square to ensure symmetry. Clamp it and remove the triangle of waste with a chisel. Then, working from each side, and towards the middle, chisel down and out to the edge in one movement. Do not press hard. This should not become heavy work, otherwise the carving will be angular and pinched. Cut in from the opposite side, subtly adjusting the line to merge in the middle. When the curve on the outer face is complete, saw a slot downwards just beyond the shoulder of the profile, and complete the shaping. Leave the carving freshly cut and unsanded as it will look neater that way.

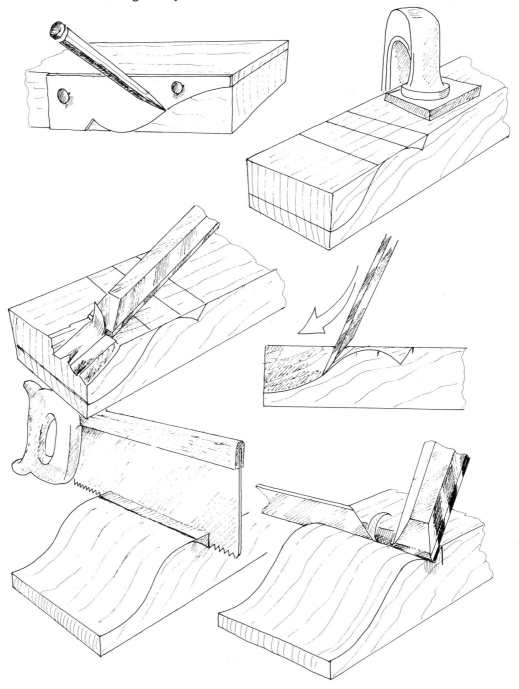

THE ROUTER

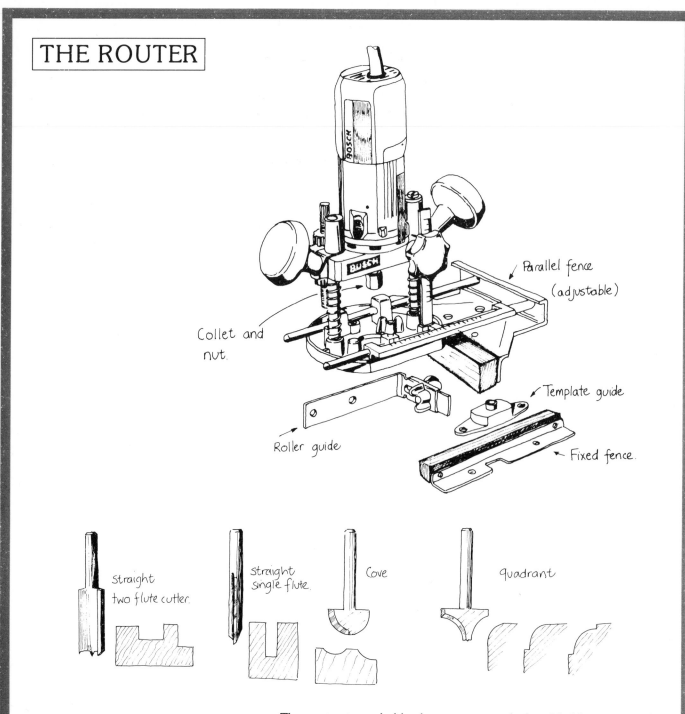

Parallel fence (adjustable)

Collet and nut.

Template guide

Roller guide

Fixed fence.

Straight two flute cutter.

Straight single flute.

Cove

Quadrant

The router is probably the most versatile hand-held power tool available to the home woodworker. You will need a router for most of the projects illustrated in this book.

The router illustrated is fitted with a 6 mm (¼ in) collet for holding the cutters. The accessories include two fences, a template and roller guides. A radius arm can be bolted to the inverted parallel fence.

A range of tools is shown. Their cutting profiles vary according to the depth to which the tool is plunged.

The tools are changed as illustrated. Ensure there is sufficient shank held in the collet, and tighten up hard the clamping nut on the shank of the new cutter. Tighten up all the other nuts and bolts on the router before it is used, otherwise they will shake loose.

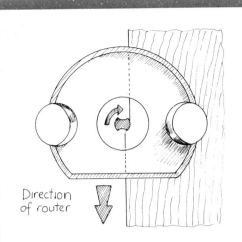

Direction of router

Pull the router against the rotation of the tool as illustrated. If you use it the other way, it leaves an unsatisfactory finish and is difficult to control. When working without a fence, use a minimum depth setting.

Scorching is caused either by a blunt tool, too high a rate of feed, or the waste chippings being prevented from falling free. Where there is a danger of scorching the wood (morticing and grooving), plunge the router in short steps, and clear the groove with light passes. Buy carbide-tipped tools for the straight cutters and high speed steel cutters, which can be sharpened with a slip stone, for those in less frequent use. Use a 6 mm (¼ in) two-flute cutter for template work, and an 8 mm (⅜ in) single flute for morticing.

■ Using the Router

1. Secure the workpiece to the bench or trestle.
2. Pre-set the depth stop, and arrange the electric cable so it is clear of the path of the router.
3. Wear safety glasses and ear mufflers if you have them.
4. Start the router and plunge it to the desired depth. Lock the plunge mechanism by twisting the right grip.
5. Slowly draw the router along the wood. Listen to the motor, and reduce the rate of cut if the motor speed drops or the tool scorches the wood.
6. When the routing is finished, release the plunge mechanism before switching off the router. Do not carry or adjust the router until the tool has finished rotating.

The router can be used to accomplish all of the woodworking functions illustrated. The diagrams show how the router is set up to obtain these results.

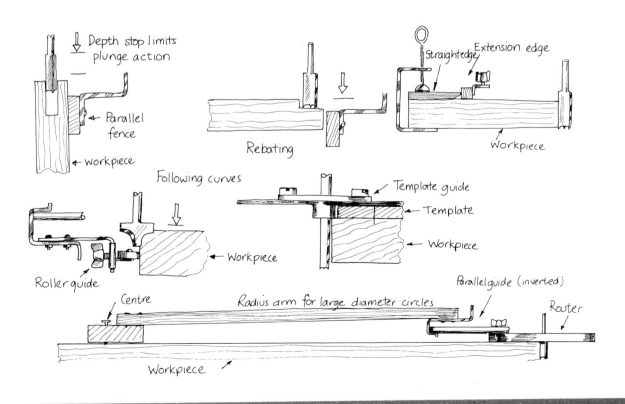

Depth stop limits plunge action — Parallel fence — Workpiece

Rebating

Straightedge — Extension edge — Workpiece

Following curves — Template guide — Template — Workpiece

Roller guide — Workpiece

Centre — Radius arm for large diameter circles — Parallel guide (inverted) — Router — Workpiece

MONK'S SEAT

THIS seat also serves as a table. The substantial base framework is similar to the bench on page 22 except that the armrests are stub tenoned (see page 30) to both front and back legs, and extend behind the back legs, where they hold the pivots for the top. The top is circular, with two crossed boards tenoned into the outer rim for strength. Two battens fastened across the top hold the pivots located in the ends of the armrests.

MONK'S BENCH

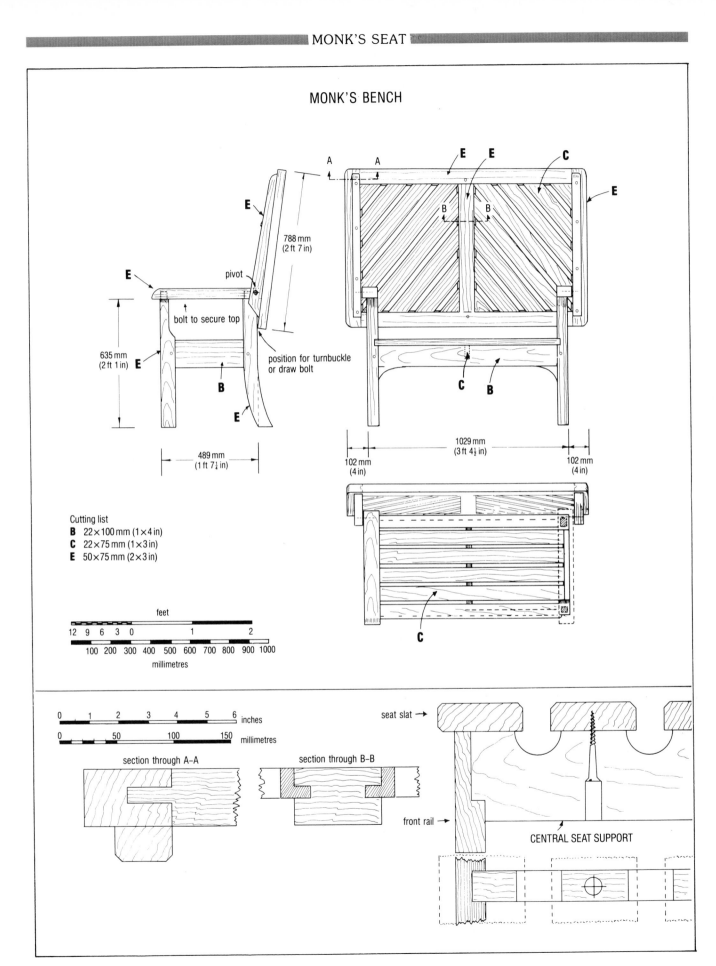

788 mm
(2 ft 7 in)

E

pivot

bolt to secure top

position for turnbuckle
or draw bolt

635 mm
(2 ft 1 in)

489 mm
(1 ft 7¼ in)

A   A

E   E   C

E

B   B

C   B

1029 mm
(3 ft 4½ in)

102 mm
(4 in)

102 mm
(4 in)

C

Cutting list
B 22×100 mm (1×4 in)
C 22×75 mm (1×3 in)
E 50×75 mm (2×3 in)

feet
12 9 6 3 0   1   2

100 200 300 400 500 600 700 800 900 1000
millimetres

0   1   2   3   4   5   6 inches
0   50   100   150 millimetres

section through A–A

section through B–B

seat slat →

front rail →

CENTRAL SEAT SUPPORT

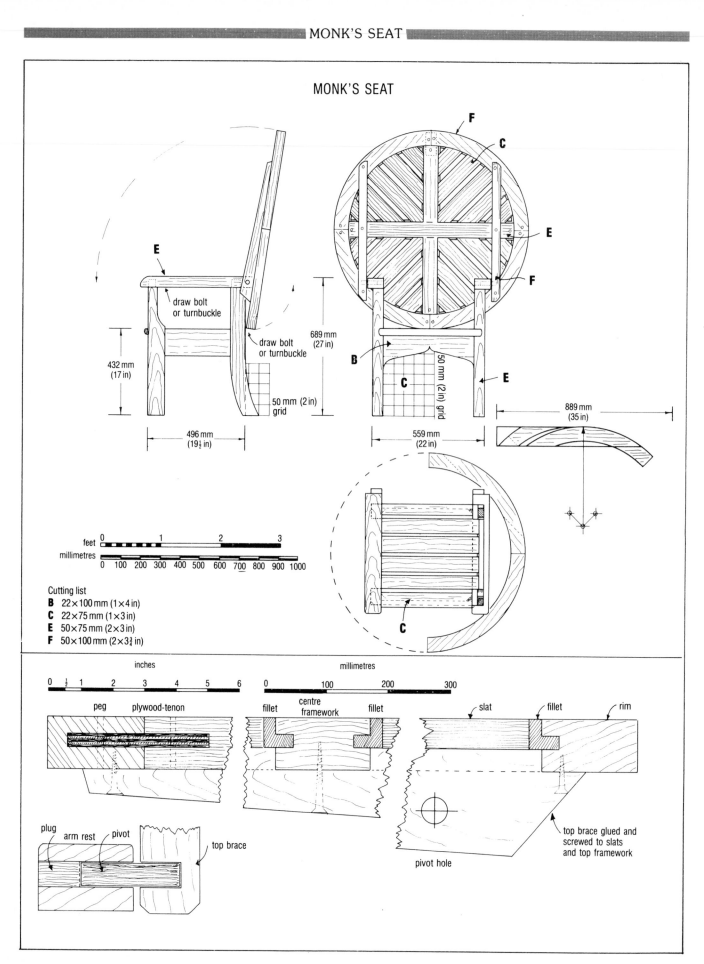

MONK'S SEAT

draw bolt
or turnbuckle

draw bolt
or turnbuckle

E

F

C

E

F

B

C

E

432 mm
(17 in)

689 mm
(27 in)

50 mm (2 in)
grid

50 mm (2 in) grid

496 mm
(19½ in)

559 mm
(22 in)

889 mm
(35 in)

feet 0 1 2 3

millimetres 0 100 200 300 400 500 600 700 800 900 1000

Cutting list
B 22×100 mm (1×4 in)
C 22×75 mm (1×3 in)
E 50×75 mm (2×3 in)
F 50×100 mm (2×3¾ in)

inches

0 ½ 1 2 3 4 5 6

millimetres

0 100 200 300

peg   plywood-tenon

fillet   centre framework   fillet

slat   fillet   rim

plug
arm rest   pivot
top brace

pivot hole

top brace glued and
screwed to slats
and top framework

Construction

■ **Base**

Make the side frames with armrests first, then the front and back rails, and backrest. Next, make the seat slats, and assemble. Cut the legs to length, make the curve to the back legs, and cut the mortices and the stub tenons at their tops. Fit the armrests, and slide in the seat slats when the second framework end is glued togther.

■ **Top Frame**

If you do not have a router bench for copy routing, you will either have to make a special router jig for cutting out the top framework or the outer and inner circles can be cut once the pieces are joined up, before grooving and glueing.

The outer frame is made from four identical pieces, jigsawn to shape and machined. Note that the outer frame can be made economically by cutting and joining the plank to give it a greater effective width. Cut the butt joints at the ends. They must be clean, square and accurate, so that when the four pieces are laid together they form a circle. Number off the pairs of joints, and clearly mark the face-side of each piece.

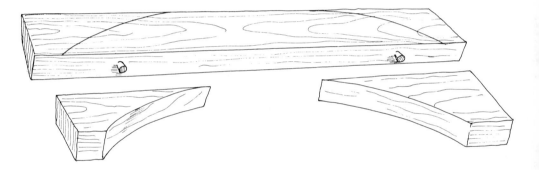

Select two sturdy straight-grained pieces of pine for the cross-pieces. Cut the cross halving joint in the centre. Assemble the outer frame, taping the mitres together, and lay it gently in position over the crossed centre pieces. Support the frame carefully, and pencil in the curves where the cross-pieces pass beneath the frame. Trim off the waste ends. Rout deep slots in the cross-piece ends, using the 8 mm (⅜ in) cutter, plunging to maximum depth. You will need to set up the router box for doing this. While you have the

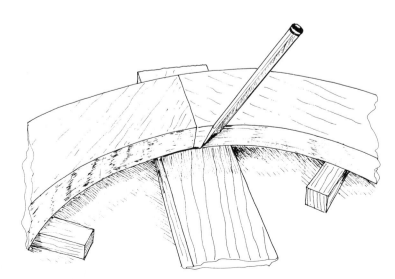

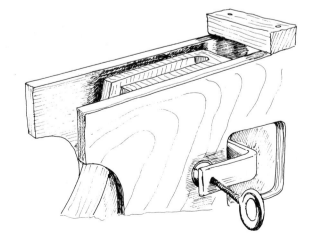

equipment set up, rout out slots in the ends of each frame member, running the slots deep into the ends of the frame, but stopping them short of the outer edge. Now, before glueing up the centre cross-halving joint, run the groove round the inside edge of the frame, and around each edge of the centre cross for the top slats. Glue up the centre cross-halving, then fit and glue a plywood tongue in the end of each arm of the cross. When the glue is dry, trim the tenons until the outer frames slide over them and fit together. Drill a peg hole through each joint in the outer frame, misaligning the hole in the tongue to pull the outer frame together.

Outer frame.

.Mortice width equal to ½ cross piece, less grooves.

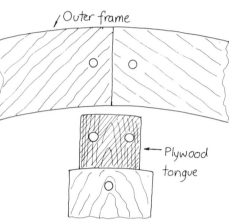

Outer frame

Plywood tongue

■ Fitting the Slats

Now, taking a quadrant at a time, lay the slats in position under the pegged up framework, and pencil in the shoulder for each slat. Trim them roughly on the router board, and complete accurate shaping with a chisel. Make up a short length of filler piece and glue and fit the slats in the first quadrant. Glue and peg the outer frame after the longest slats are in place. If there is difficulty in pressing the 25 mm (1 in) filler strips into the curved frame, saw a couple of sawcuts through their tongues, to help them bend. Repeat for the other three quadrants.

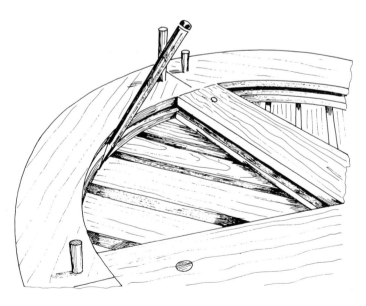

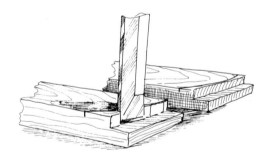

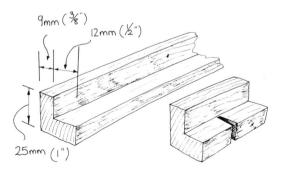

9mm (⅜")

12mm (½")

25mm (1")

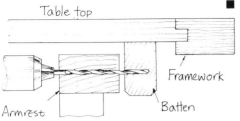

Table top
Framework
Armrest
Batten

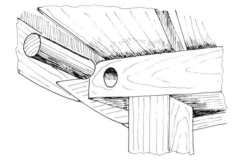

■ Pivotting the Table Top

When the top is sanded and the crevices are filled, cut and fit two strong battens to support the top. Place the top in position over the base, and clamp the battens to the top, 3 mm (⅛ in) outside the armrests. Trim the battens until they sit snugly against the rim and slats of the table top, using a dumbstick or dividers to transfer the shapes. Taper the lower edges of the battens into the shape illustrated in the plans, glue and screw them in place. When you have measured and are sure everything is correct, drill a 3 mm (⅛ in) hole and see if the table pivots on two nails. If it does, drill right through the tabletop armrest with a 18 mm (¾ in) bit, and drill on into the sides of the batten, stopping as soon as the bit has centred in the nail hole. Now fit a 25 mm (1 in) bit and bore out the recesses for the pivot. This needs to be oversize, because the joint must always be free. When the top is ready and in position, insert a 18 mm (¾ in) dowel through the batten into the armrest, and fix it to the batten with a countersunk screw. Assemble the table after painting it, and fasten the turnbuckle to the back legs to hold the table in its upright position.

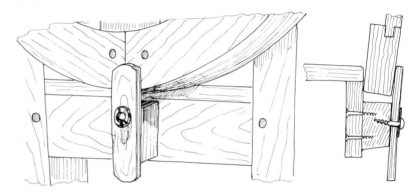

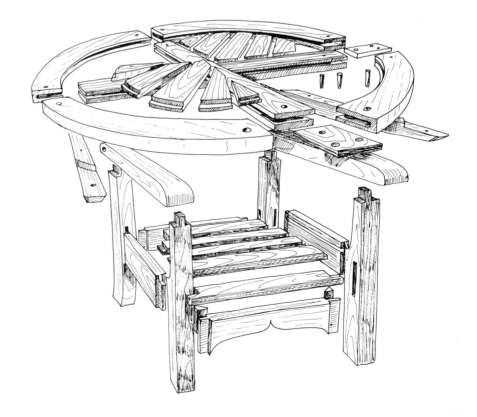

Nail Types

As a rough guide when selecting a nail, choose a nail three times longer than the thickness of the wood you are nailing.

■ Panel Pins

These do not hold well, but you can conceal them by punching their heads below the surface of the wood, and filling the hole with weatherproof stopping. The punch should be the same size as the panel pinhead. Hold the punch as illustrated, and steady it with your little finger. Use panel pins and glue where your work will be seen.

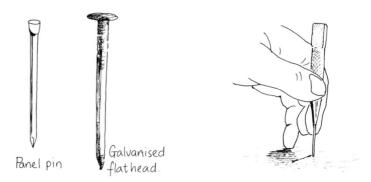

Panel pin

Galvanised flathead.

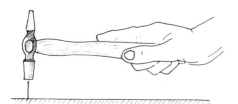

■ Galvanised Flatheads

These have greater holding power than pins, but their heads cannot be hidden. Use them in conjunction with glue in areas where they will not be noticed.

Select a large hammer for hitting large nails, and a small pin hammer for small nails and panel pins. Hold the hammer as illustrated, moving your hand downwards slightly as the nail is hammered home.

Support your work with a heavy weight held directly behind the nail. If you are worried that the wood will split, pre-drill it first, using a drill of the same size as the nail, or cut the head off a similar nail and use it as a drill.

Nailing Problems

The hammer slips off the nail: Check that you are holding the hammer correctly. Clean the face of the hammer with wire wool or sandpaper.

Slippery glue makes it difficult to nail two pieces together accurately: Drive the nail through the top board, and apply the glue once the nail points out of the other side, where it will prevent the wood from sliding about.

Removing nails: The main problem in removing a freshly driven nail is to avoid bruising the surface surrounding the nail. If you can see the nail is bending, stop hammering and pull it out before things get worse. Use nail pincers to pull nails out, resting them against a wood offcut to protect the wood surface. If the nail is driven right in, it is often easiest to lever the two pieces of wood apart with an old chisel or a floorboard lifting tool, and extract the nail once they are separated. Where this is impossible, excavate around the nail until you can lever it upright with a screwdriver, bearing against a pad of wood.

SCREWING

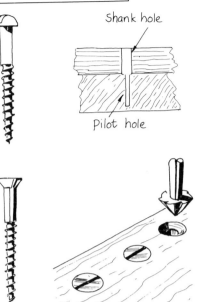

Shank hole

Pilot hole

Always pre-drill the wood before driving in a screw.

■ Roundhead Screws

These are available in brass, steel and stainless steel. Use, perhaps with a small washer slipped under the head, when the screw is counterbored into soft wood. The flat underside of the head and the washer prevent the wood from splitting. Roundhead screws need two holes before they can be used – a pilot hole the depth of the screw, which is drilled first, then a shank hole to allow the top third of the screw to pass through the wood freely.

■ Countersunk Screws

These are also available in brass, steel and stainless steel. They are used for fastening hinges and handles and where the screwheads will be seen. As countersunk screws are meant to be set flush into the wood, in addition to drilling a pilot and shank hole, you will have to bore a conical recess using a conical bit. Countersink carefully – overlarge recesses look ugly. Line up the screwheads parallel to the nearest straight line.

■ Chipboard Screws

Chipboard screws are zincplated, and have a sharp point and bold thread which stops short of the head, enabling the screw to pull the wood together. They are very quick and easy to use, providing you pre-drill an adequate pilot hole the depth of the shank. They are ideal as a substitute for clamping when glueing up a piece of work, but should not be used where the heads will be seen.

Counterboring

This is often necessary when screwing through a deep framework, such as when fastening a table top. Rather than buy very long and expensive screws, first drill a large diameter hole, then the pilot and shank hole as illustrated. Use roundhead or countersunk screws to pull the pieces together.

A variation is illustrated opposite, which allows the top plank some movement for shrinkage, and the fastening room to bend slightly as the top shrinks and swells. Fill the holes with silicone sealer before screwing the components together, to prevent moisture from accumulating.

Screwing Problems

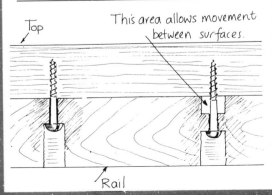

Top

This area allows movement between surfaces.

Rail

Screw slots are damaged: This is because the wrong-sized screwdriver has been used, or the pilot or shank hole is the incorrect size or depth. In either case, excessive force has been needed to turn the screw, which has damaged the slot. Always use a screwdriver of the same width as the screw head, keep the point of the screwdriver square and flat, and pre-drill holes of adequate size.

Wood is damaged by the screwdriver: Either the screwdriver is too wide, and scoring the wood as it rotates, or the screwdriver is slipping because too much force is required to turn the screw. Change screwdrivers, or remove the screws and re-drill the screw holes.

TREE SEAT

THE tree seat is simple to prefabricate in the workshop, but some care is needed in assembling it around the tree. It is a modular design, and only supports itself when all the units are fixed together. A small bench, such as a workmate, erected by the tree, will be a great help to work on.

Site work is often troublesome. Spend time laying out your tools, and organising them before beginning work, and if, because of the unusual conditions in which you are woodworking, you find that the pieces are falling about all over the place, and there are not enough hands to hold them, stop and rethink your strategy for building the seat and supporting it. This seat will be attractive and comfortable if it is put together properly, but it will be disappointing if it is asymmetrical or bodged, and it might collapse.

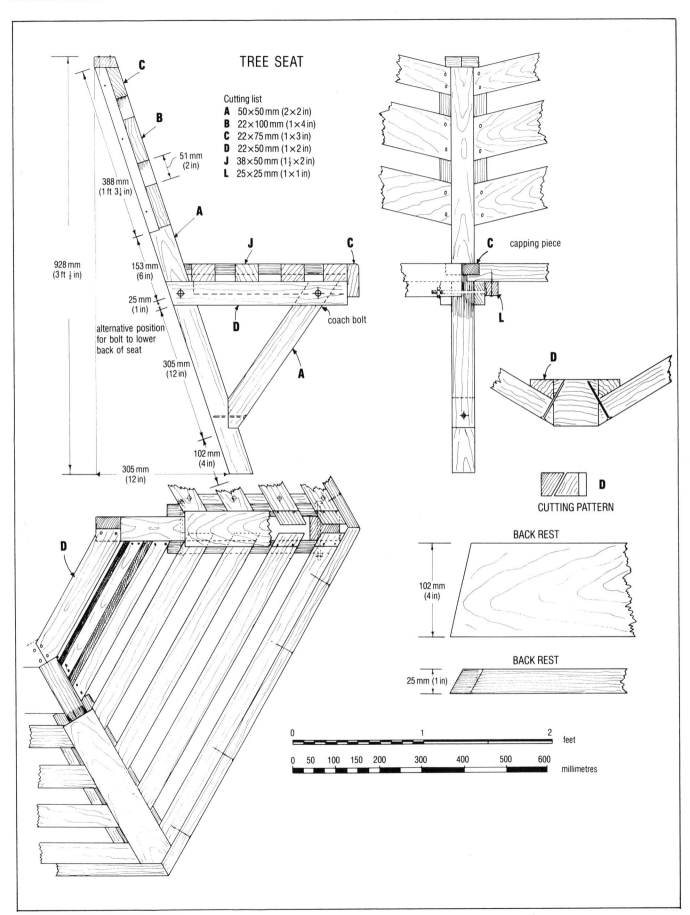

TREE SEAT

Cutting list
A 50×50 mm (2×2 in)
B 22×100 mm (1×4 in)
C 22×75 mm (1×3 in)
D 22×50 mm (1×2 in)
J 38×50 mm (1½×2 in)
L 25×25 mm (1×1 in)

51 mm (2 in)

388 mm (1 ft 3¼ in)

928 mm (3 ft ½ in)

153 mm (6 in)

25 mm (1 in)

alternative position for bolt to lower back of seat

305 mm (12 in)

305 mm (12 in)

102 mm (4 in)

coach bolt

capping piece

CUTTING PATTERN

BACK REST

102 mm (4 in)

BACK REST

25 mm (1 in)

0   1   2   feet

0 50 100 150 200   300   400   500 600   millimetres

93

Construction

The design shows a seat with six legs, made up of three seat modules with two legs each, joined to each other by backrests and seat slats. The components of each module are pre–cut, using cardboard marking and drilling templates. The slats that connect the modules are cut and fitted on site.

■ Prefabrication

Cut the legs to length and, depending on the ground and root pattern round the tree, add a little extra to the ends so they can be adjusted to height. Take the legs one at a time, and saw out the notch to support the seat brace. Glue and bolt the seat supports, and then slip in the brace. Bolt it at the top, and nail and glue it into the notch. Bevel the outer edges of the backrest support to the appropriate angle, then glue and nail it to the back of the legs. Trim the tops.

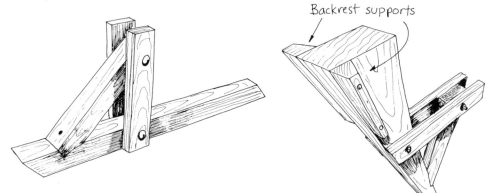

Backrest supports

When the legs are ready, tack temporary battens to hold the first pair apart at their correct splay. Measure and then cut the three back slats for each section, noting that the end cuts are angled in both planes, then glue and nail them in place. When the glue is dry, make a template for the seat units. Cut the slats to length and prefabricate the seat units, nailing and glueing the two end braces in position beneath them. Nail and glue in the seat units for the three completed modules.

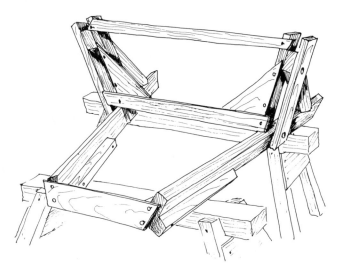

■ Assembly

Nail temporary battens to the top of each module to hold them to the tree. Use a spirit level to check that each module is level and the same height as the one next to it. Adjust and trim them until they are. Now tack battens between the modules, and screw and glue the seat and backrest. Fit the capping pieces at the front edge of the seat and over the top of the legs.

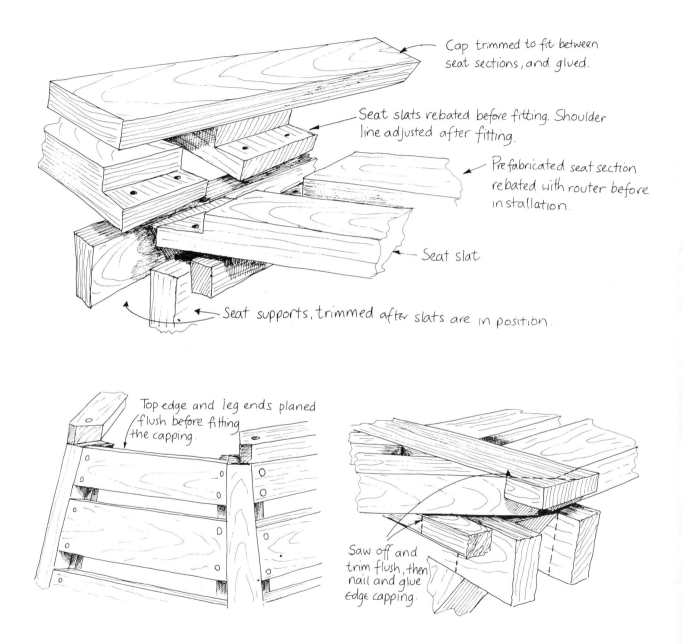

Cap trimmed to fit between seat sections, and glued.

Seat slats rebated before fitting. Shoulder line adjusted after fitting.

Prefabricated seat section rebated with router before installation.

Seat slat

Seat supports, trimmed after slats are in position.

Top edge and leg ends planed flush before fitting the capping.

Saw off and trim flush, then nail and glue edge capping.

■ Treating

Some parts of this seat will always be in the shade and, once in place, it will not be easy to move it, so treat every piece of wood with preservative before assembly. In particular, soak each freshly sawn end in a basin of preservative for three minutes to prolong the life of the seat.

SUN LOUNGER

THE tilt of the slatted headrest of this sun lounger is adjustable. Its supporting arms rest on a rack, hidden behind the front legs. The wheels can be obtained from the suppliers listed in the back of the book.

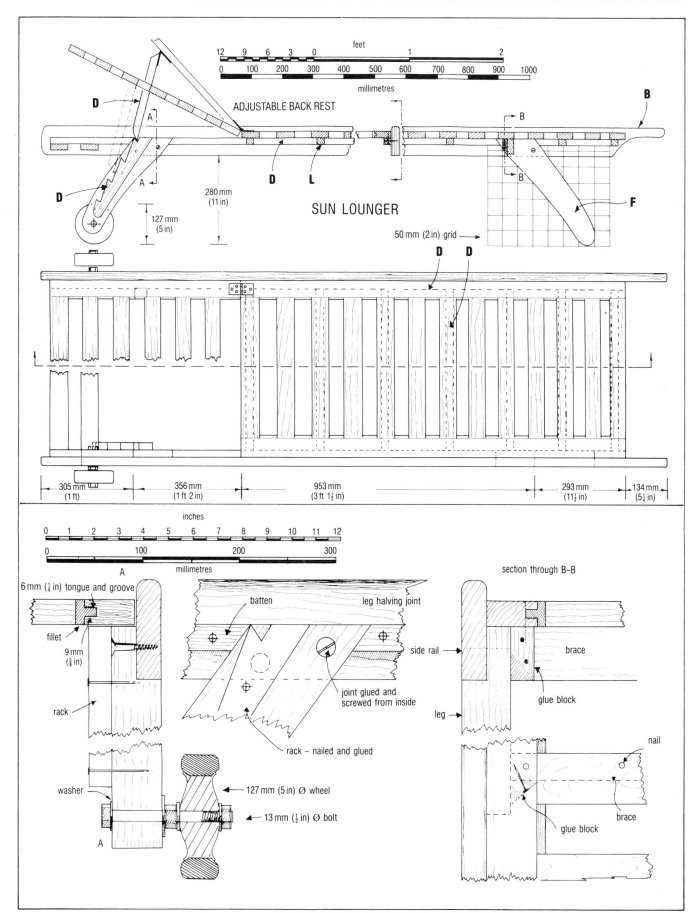

ADJUSTABLE BACK REST

feet

12 9 6 3 0   1   2

0   100 200 300 400 500 600 700 800 900 1000

millimetres

SUN LOUNGER

280 mm
(11 in)

127 mm
(5 in)

50 mm (2 in) grid

305 mm
(1 ft)

356 mm
(1 ft 2 in)

953 mm
(3 ft 1½ in)

293 mm
(11½ in)

134 mm
(5¼ in)

inches

0 1 2 3 4 5 6 7 8 9 10 11 12

0   100   200   300

millimetres

A

section through B–B

6 mm (¼ in) tongue and groove

fillet

9 mm
(⅜ in)

rack

batten

leg halving joint

joint glued and
screwed from inside

rack – nailed and glued

side rail

brace

glue block

leg

washer

127 mm (5 in) Ø wheel

13 mm (½ in) Ø bolt

A

nail

brace

glue block

Construction

Cut the side beams to length. Shape the handles with a jigsaw. Chisel and then plane a radius on the top edges, and round the front edges of the side beams.

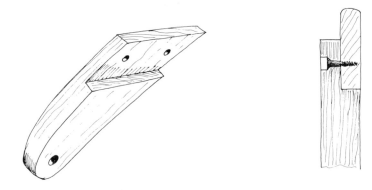

■ Battens

Fit the two 25 mm (1 in) battens to the inside of the side beams. They are set below the top edges of the beams. Glue and nail them in position. Glueing is made easier if you drive the nails into the batten, with their points just emerging through the other side, where they will provide a key, and stop the battens slipping about. (See plans.)

■ Legs

Cut out the legs for the lounger, and saw out the recess in each leg to fit around the side beams. Counterbore and then screw the legs into position onto the side beams, and drill the front legs for the axles.

■ Slatted Supports

Make up the slatted headrest and the main slatted body support. Groove the side members and slot in the transverse battens, adding filler pieces between them. Build the sections separately on a board, holding the side beams in position with blocks. When the transverse slats are in position, tighten them together with wedges until the glue is dry.

Nail and glue on the main section, and then fit the head support. Link the two slatted sections with a pair of back flap hinges, as illustrated. Install the remaining transverse battens at the front end, fitting them to the underside of the 25 mm (1 in) batten glued to the edge of the side beams.

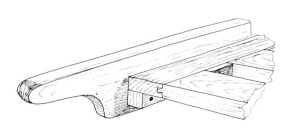

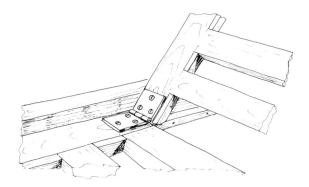

■ Pawl and Rack

Cut out the two racks, and glue and pin them to the inside of the legs and side beams. Cut out and fit the two pawls, join them with a strut, and hinge them to the headrest.

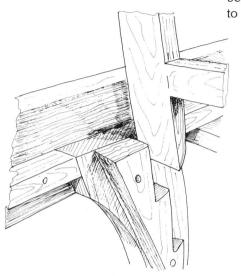

■ Wheels

The wheels are fitted as illustrated. Use large, close-fitting washers and tighten up the holding nut against a pin inserted through the bolt to prevent the axle from working loose.

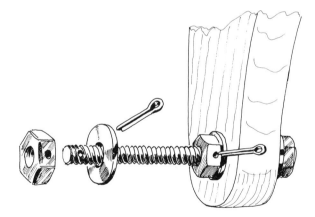

■ Finishing

This sun lounger can either be finished with a transparent finish, or with paint. If it is going to be painted, fill the screw holes with weatherproof filler, and apply two coats of microporous paint. A transparent epoxy finish will also look good. For this, the screw holes will have to be plugged with short wooden plugs. These can be bought, but they are very easy to make with a plug cutting tool, fitted into an electric drill. It is easier to control the drill if it is mounted on a drill stand. Lever the plugs free from the scrap wood with a screwdriver, apply glue to the plug, align its grain, and tap it home with a hammer.

Sand the lounger smooth, and fill all the holes and crevices with thickened epoxy resin, before applying three coats of resin. Finish with an ultraviolet inhibiting varnish.

PLANTERS

A PLANTER is a box full of earth. The designs here incorporate an inner plywood box to hold the earth, so the planters can be made successfully from pine. Teak, oak or sequoia can also be used. Between the inner and outer planter there is an airgap for ventilation.

The planters are panelled with 25 mm (1 in) thick solid pine, held in a wooden framework of legs and rails, morticed and tenoned together. The panels are made from solid wood, which shrink and expand with changes in humidity, so they are slotted into grooves in the retaining frame, and not glued. The base consists of diagonal slats on which the inner box stands.

Two planters are illustrated. 'A' has turned finials, and fielded panels, 'B' has fluted legs and flat panels. If you have a lathe, or can adapt your electric drill to make one, simple instructions for turning the finials are included on page 105. If you do not have access to a lathe, make planter 'B'. From a woodworking point of view this is a more demanding alternative, but the results will be pleasing, unusual, and attractive. In both cases, the trellis sits on top of the legs.

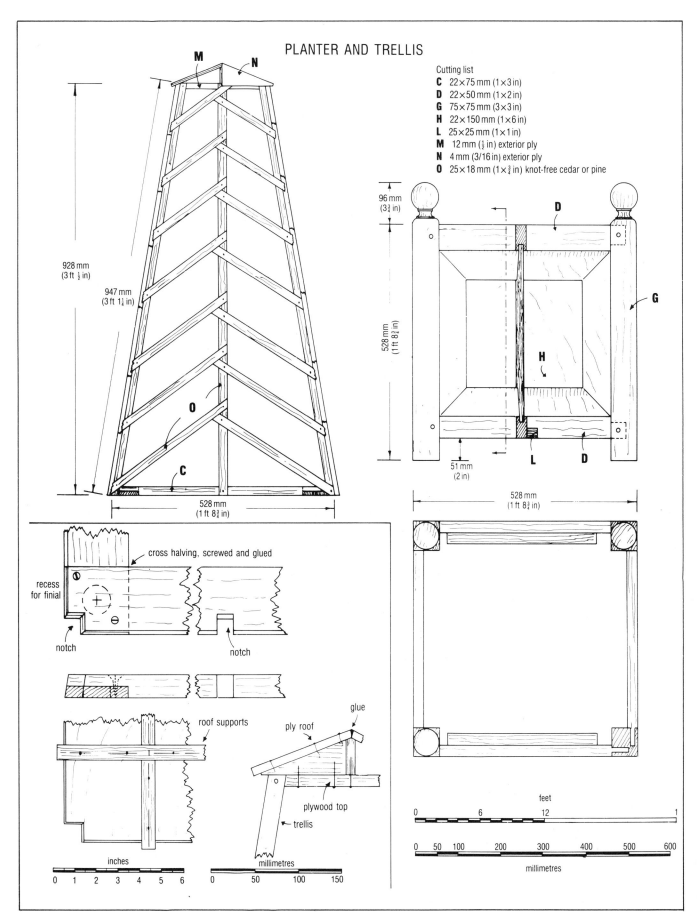

PLANTER AND TRELLIS

Cutting list
C 22×75 mm (1×3 in)
D 22×50 mm (1×2 in)
G 75×75 mm (3×3 in)
H 22×150 mm (1×6 in)
L 25×25 mm (1×1 in)
M 12 mm (½ in) exterior ply
N 4 mm (3/16 in) exterior ply
O 25×18 mm (1×¾ in) knot-free cedar or pine

928 mm (3 ft ½ in)

947 mm (3 ft 1¼ in)

528 mm (1 ft 8¾ in)

96 mm (3¾ in)

528 mm (1 ft 8¾ in)

51 mm (2 in)

528 mm (1 ft 8¾ in)

cross halving, screwed and glued

recess for finial

notch

notch

roof supports

ply roof

glue

plywood top

trellis

inches
0 1 2 3 4 5 6

millimetres
0 50 100 150

feet
0 6 12 1

0 50 100 200 300 400 500 600

millimetres

Construction

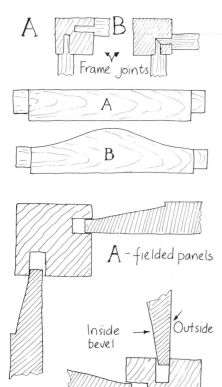

A · B

Frame joints

A

B

A - fielded panels

Inside
bevel → Outside

B

The order of construction for both planters is the same. Variations are noted here, then dealt with in more detail later in this section.

■ Legs

Plunge out the mortices, and rout the grooves which are stopped in the mortices, before turning or shaping the legs. Note that the position of the mortices and grooves vary with the two designs. The mortices in the legs of planter 'B' are set well into the inside corner of the box, unlike those of 'A', which are close to the outside edge of the square leg.

When the mortices and panel grooves are cut, shape the tops of the legs, and champher the edges where appropriate. Now make up the rails, grooving and tenoning them as described on page 27. Shape the tops of the rails.

Glue two 25 mm (1 in) square battens, opposite each other, onto the inside bottom edges of the lower rails, to support the inner box.

■ Panels

Use epoxy resin to glue together enough boards to make up the panels. Remember that with this box, the problems will not be those of shrinkage, but expansion. Once the box is outside, the wood will never again be as dry as it is now. Almost all the movement will be over the width of the board.

Make the panel wide enough to fill the space in the framework, entering the groove by about 3 mm (⅛ in) on each side; but there should be at least 9 mm (⅜ in) additional depth in the groove to accommodate swelling caused by moisture take-up. When the panel is cut to exact size, the edges can be planed down to fit into the framework groove. Bevel the inside edges of the panels for planter 'B', and plane the outside flat (as illustrated). Plane the panels flat inside and outside for 'A', and then mark the outside in preparation for fielding the panel.

■ Fielding

If you have an electric planer, then the fielding operation is straightforward. Set up the guides and plane the bevelled rebate across the grain first, and then with the grain. Alternatively, use the shelving routing jig, fitting a 12 mm (½ in) or 16 mm (¾ in) cutter in the router and plunging the router to a fixed 9 mm (⅜ in) setting. Remove the routing marks with a belt sander.

■ Assembling the Planter

Assemble the box, glueing it with epoxy resin and pegging the joints. Take care not to run glue onto the panels which should be centred in the frames. When you have finished glueing up the planter, drive a panel pin into the inside edge of the four top rails at their centres to hold the panel central.

■ Inner Box

This is very simple to make. Use 6 mm (¼ in) exterior plywood, and 12 mm × 25 mm (½ in × 1 in) pine battens. Staple and glue the battens, as illustrated. Add additional lengths of pine strip for spacers, and when the box is ready, drop it into the planter, resting it on four diagonal slats glued across the inside. Drill some small drainage holes near the bottom of the box. A few coats of linseed oil will help preserve the box from deterioration.

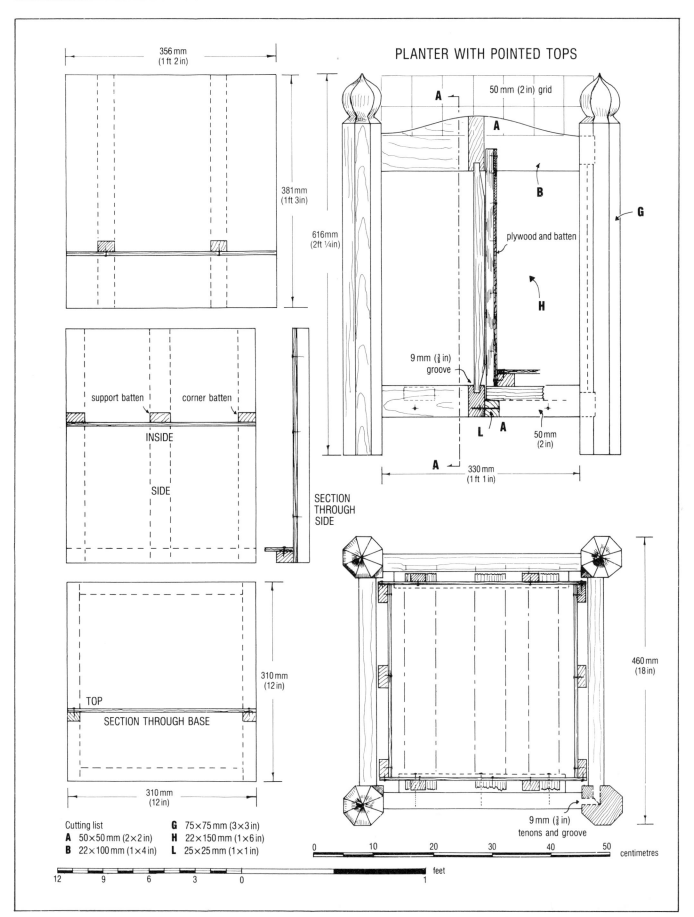

356 mm
(1 ft 2 in)

381 mm
(1 ft 3 in)

616 mm
(2 ft ¼ in)

support batten

corner batten

INSIDE

SIDE

SECTION
THROUGH
SIDE

TOP

SECTION THROUGH BASE

310 mm
(12 in)

310 mm
(12 in)

PLANTER WITH POINTED TOPS

50 mm (2 in) grid

A

A

B

G

plywood and batten

H

9 mm (⅜ in)
groove

L A

50 mm
(2 in)

A

330 mm
(1 ft 1 in)

460 mm
(18 in)

9 mm (⅜ in)
tenons and groove

Cutting list
A 50×50 mm (2×2 in)
B 22×100 mm (1×4 in)
G 75×75 mm (3×3 in)
H 22×150 mm (1×6 in)
L 25×25 mm (1×1 in)

0   10   20   30   40   50
centimetres

12   9   6   3   0   1   feet

TURNING

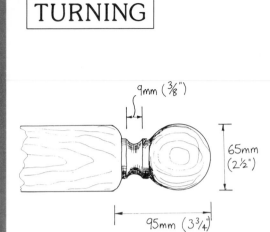

9mm (3/8")

65mm (2½")

95mm (3¾")

If you are unfamiliar with the techniques of turning, the following tips will help you to turn the end finials for planter 'A'.

You should have three types of turning tools: a gouge or two, at least two very sharp knife-like chisels, honed on both edges, and a couple of scrapers. The gouges and the scrapers are sharpened on a grindstone, and are left with a rough, jagged edge. They are not honed. The knives are sharpened to a keen edge, like a penknife (but when sharpening them, remember to hone the sides in the ratio of about 5:1, otherwise you will never arrive at a particularly sharp edge).

One of your knives will be ground square to the shank of the tool. This is the parting chisel, used for cutting straight sided grooves, or for cutting off work when it is finished. The others are sharpened at about 45° and are for smoothing rough-cut cylinders and cutting convex shapes. The gouges are for roughing wood into a cylinder prior to shaping, and for sinking radiused recesses in the wood. The scrapers can be used for shaping, but they tear the wood apart, and leave a very rough finish.

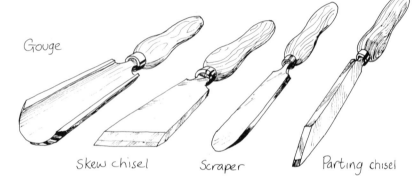

Gouge

Skew chisel   Scraper   Parting chisel

■ Roughing

Cut the legs to length, leaving about 6 mm (¼ mm) extra at one end. Find the centre at each end (by diagonals) and mark the centre with a punch. Tap the bottom of the leg into the teeth of the headstock (the rotating head) and hold the other end with the tailstock, winding the point up tight into the mark, and then releasing it half a turn to allow the leg to revolve freely. Dot a drip of oil onto the point of the tailstock centrebit for lubrication.

Pencil in the shoulder of the finial, and the top at the tailstock end. Then start the lathe. With the big gouge held tightly with both hands at the angle illustrated, press it against the tool rest and lightly cut into the shoulder mark. Now pull the tool along the tool rest towards the tailstock. Repeat, until the end part of the leg is rough and cylindrical.

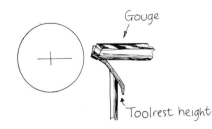

Gouge

Toolrest height

Parting chisel

Toolrest height

■ Shaping

Now use the parting tool to cut a shallow groove just above the shoulder. Widen the grove by moving the tool along the toolrest and starting again the gentle tilting motion which makes it such a pleasant and effective tool to use. (Lift the handle to lower the point as the tool bites deeper into the centre). Now cut the radius into the bottom of the groove. Practise this manoeuvre with the lathe switched off before you do any cutting. Take the small gouge and, tilting it on its side, and holding it very tightly to the tool rest, move it into the wood, and twist it 10°–15° in a clockwise direction. Stop in the middle of the groove, and repeat in the other direction to finish.

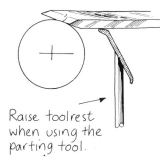

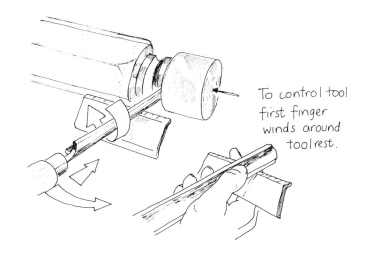

To control tool first finger winds around toolrest.

Raise toolrest when using the parting tool.

■ Rounding the Finial

Now take the largest skew chisel, raise the tool rest until it is level with the top of the short cylinder which you are about to shape into the finial and rest the chisel flat against the centre of the cylinder. Holding it tight, twist it slightly in an anti-clockwise direction until the cutting edge removes a fine shaving. Move the chisel along the cylinder, and as you get to the edge, twist it a bit more until it cuts off the hard-edged corner. This last manoeuvre is what is needed to round off the top and bottom of the finial, so practise the twisting and cutting operation until you feel in control of the tool. If the work begins to chatter, you are either trying to slice off too much wood, or the tailstock needs tightening. Repeat at the top end of the leg to complete the finial.

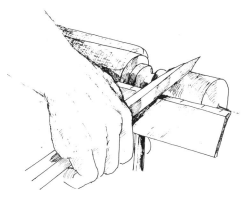

■ Fluting Legs

Although a fluted leg may look like a regular polygon in section, in fact the two inner faces which comprise the framework are at right angles to each other, and should be left like that when the rest of the leg is shaped.

The frame has to be assembled before the legs can be fluted. Then mark off one of the legs where the shoulders of the side frame meet it. Mark the lines with a pencil. The leg outside the lines can be bevelled into the polygon, but inside the line they must not be touched. Run a pencil line down the leg to extend the frame line, then, marking from both the bottom and the top, draw in the largest possible circle on the ends, and mark in the faces for the figure. Place the leg in the vice, and plane down to these marked faces.

Repeat with the remaining legs.

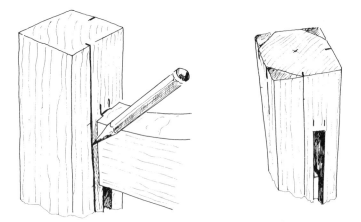

■ Shaping the Top

Mark off the shoulder for the finial, by wrapping a strip of masking tape round the leg, 100 mm (4 in) from the top. Draw a second line 12 mm (½ in) above it. Place the leg in the vice, and between these two lines, cut a light saw cut 12 mm (½ in) deep right round the leg. Now chisel out the groove, working in from both lines and cutting round the leg.

The top of the finial is marked off in the same way. Saw the points for the top, then, with the leg held upright in the vice, carefully chisel each facet with a sweep up to the top. Try to avoid over sandpapering the finished carving, it will probably look neater if the carving errors and irregularities are left as they are.

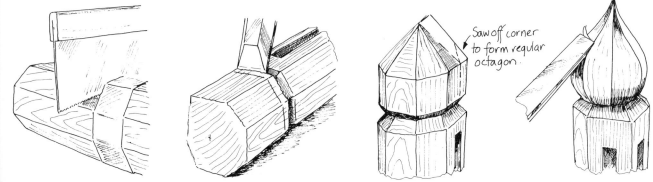

Saw off corner to form regular octagon.

MAKING A TRELLIS

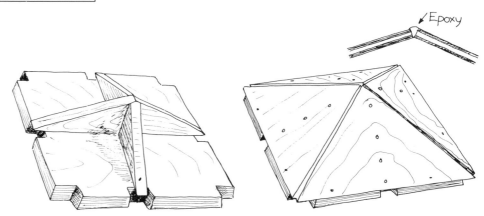

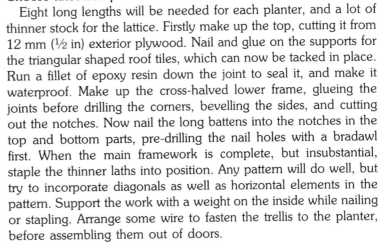

Press bradawl into wood with point at right angles to avoid splitting grain.

Choose knot-free pine or cedar for the trellis.

Eight long lengths will be needed for each planter, and a lot of thinner stock for the lattice. Firstly make up the top, cutting it from 12 mm (½ in) exterior plywood. Nail and glue on the supports for the triangular shaped roof tiles, which can now be tacked in place. Run a fillet of epoxy resin down the joint to seal it, and make it waterproof. Make up the cross-halved lower frame, glueing the joints before drilling the corners, bevelling the sides, and cutting out the notches. Now nail the long battens into the notches in the top and bottom parts, pre-drilling the nail holes with a bradawl first. When the main framework is complete, but insubstantial, staple the thinner laths into position. Any pattern will do well, but try to incorporate diagonals as well as horizontal elements in the pattern. Support the work with a weight on the inside while nailing or stapling. Arrange some wire to fasten the trellis to the planter, before assembling them out of doors.

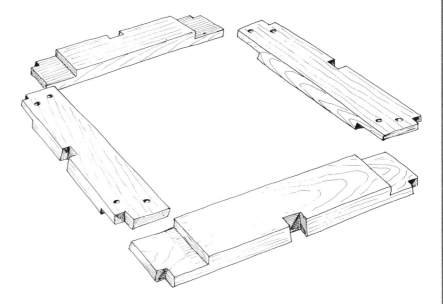

CRICKET TABLE

THIS is a traditional English country table. Its top is thick and heavy, and in
time it will split, wear at the edge and joints, and rot in places. It is strong,
practical, a useful size and never rocks.

The top is glued together and screwed from the underside. The triangular
upper framework is morticed together. The rails are tenoned straight into the
legs, with sloped shoulders to splay the legs, which are tapered gracefully
from just below the lower tier. The legs are planed to the section illustrated.

CRICKET TABLE

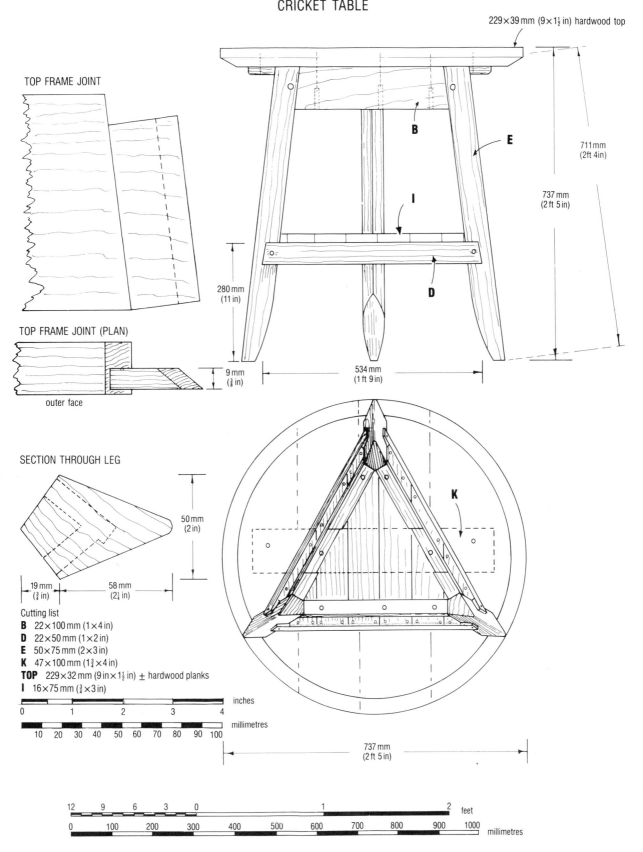

TOP FRAME JOINT

TOP FRAME JOINT (PLAN)

outer face

SECTION THROUGH LEG

229×39 mm (9×1½ in) hardwood top

B

E

I

D

711 mm
(2 ft 4 in)

737 mm
(2 ft 5 in)

280 mm
(11 in)

9 mm
(⅜ in)

534 mm
(1 ft 9 in)

50 mm
(2 in)

19 mm
(¾ in)

58 mm
(2¼ in)

K

Cutting list
B 22×100 mm (1×4 in)
D 22×50 mm (1×2 in)
E 50×75 mm (2×3 in)
K 47×100 mm (1¾×4 in)
TOP 229×32 mm (9 in×1½ in) ± hardwood planks
I 16×75 mm (¾×3 in)

inches
0   1   2   3   4

millimetres
10 20 30 40 50 60 70 80 90 100

737 mm
(2 ft 5 in)

12   9   6   3   0   1   2   feet

0   100   200   300   400   500   600   700   800   900   1000

millimetres

Construction

■ Legs and Rails

Mark off the legs from a single plank, adding 50 mm (2 in) to the top end of each one before cutting them off. This additional length makes it easier to hold the legs when they are being morticed. Transfer the tapered section illustrated above onto the ends of the legs. Pencil in the new corners for the leg, before clamping the first leg in the vice and planing it to the tapered section in the order illustrated.

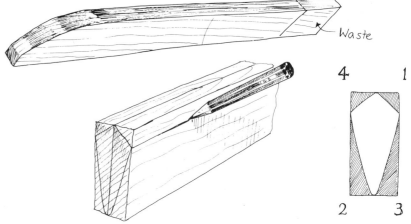

Cut the three top rails and saw the tenons, using the same sliding bevel setting for all six shoulders, and trim the sloping haunches with a chisel. Next measure the legs: from the foot, mark off the position for the mortices on the narrow inner faces of the leg. Place one leg at a time in the router box. Hold the top end with a self-tapping screw through the router box into the 50 mm (2 in) waste at the top of the leg.

Clamp the other end and raise one side of the box so that the router plunges the mortices at the correct angle. Rout all six mortices.

Take each leg in turn and, using a 9 mm (3/8 in) chisel, tap out the top and bottom of the mortice until the tenon fits tightly.

■ Assembling the Base

When all the rails fit, assemble the framework and mark off at the top edge of the side rails the angle at which the top will have to be trimmed. Use a straightedge to mark this as illustrated. Then, marking up from the floor, pencil in the position of the lower tier supports and the beginning of the leg taper. Dismantle the pieces and trim them. Glue up the table framework, pulling the mortices up with pegs as described on page 29.

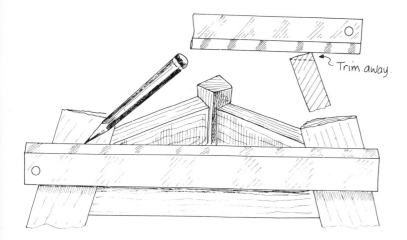

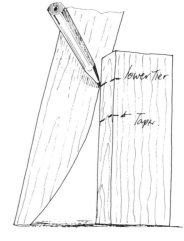

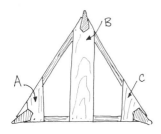

When the glue is dry, nail and glue the bottom rails, and fit the lower tier of shelving, fitting the awkward corner planks A, B, C first. The middle planks, which should be a slight wedged fit can be trimmed to length after they are fitted. Round the top edges of the lower tier with a block plane and file.

Now that the table framework is strong and steady, saw off the waste from the top of the legs and plane around the top to level it.

Lay the brace across the top rails. Mark and slot the rails to hold it, then cut the brace to length and bevel its underside with a wide chisel. Leave the rough chisel marks, glue and screw the brace in place.

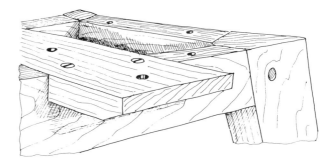

■ Assembling the Top

Glue and fit the top together on the framework. Screw through the top rails and the brace to hold it. When the glue has cured, mark and cut round the circular top with a jigsaw fitted with a fine blade, and chisel and plane a bevel on the underside of the edge. Finish with paint, oil or with dark microporous stain.

111

BUTLER'S TRAY

THE butler's tray is in two parts: a folding stand, lightly constructed of pine struts and webbing, and a mahogany tray. The sides of the tray hinge downwards when it is resting on the trestle, to form an elliptical table top. This is the only piece of furniture in this book where the surface finish has to be clean, smooth and beautiful. It need not be weatherproof, but it should be able to withstand surface damage caused by hot water or spirits. Traditionally, the tray would be made from mahogany, but good quality mahogany in the sizes needed is difficult to find, and expensive. Instead, use 12 mm (½ in) marine mahogany-faced/grade plywood. This has high quality surface veneers and a void free inner core, and can be shaped to the long gentle curves required without revealing a rough and porous end grain. However, the plies will show, and apart from painting or gilding the upper edges of the tray rim, and the inside edges of the cut-out handles, there is not much that can be done about it.

Special hinges which lock in the open position, are required; they are available from the suppliers listed on page 122.

Where the surface finish is so important, it is essential to handle your tools and the wood very carefully. Ensure that the bench is clean and smooth before laying down the mahogany boards, and do not drop things on its surface. Every blemish has to be filled or sanded smooth before finishing, so it saves time to be careful.

BUTLER'S TRAY

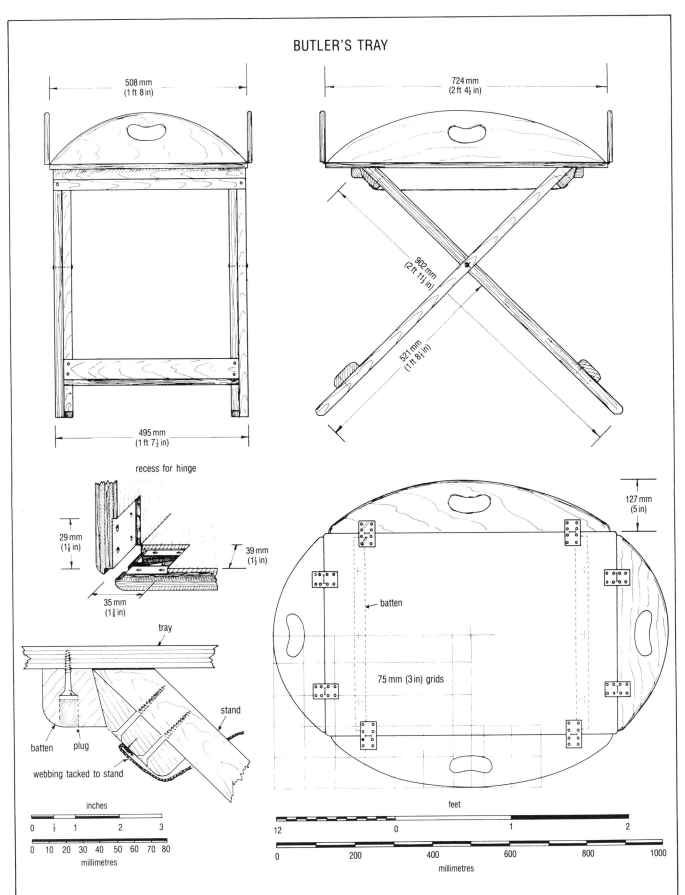

508 mm
(1 ft 8 in)

724 mm
(2 ft 4½ in)

902 mm
(2 ft 11½ in)

521 mm
(1 ft 8½ in)

495 mm
(1 ft 7½ in)

recess for hinge

29 mm
(1⅛ in)

39 mm
(1½ in)

35 mm
(1⅜ in)

127 mm
(5 in)

batten

75 mm (3 in) grids

tray

stand

batten   plug

webbing tacked to stand

inches

0   ½   1   2   3

0 10 20 30 40 50 60 70 80
millimetres

feet

12   0   1   2

0   200   400   600   800   1000
millimetres

113

Construction

■ Tray

For a small additional fee, most plywood suppliers will cut the plywood to the sizes you require, prior to the final shaping. It will make things easier if they do, because plywood is cumbersome and heavy to handle, and quite difficult to cut by hand. If you have to saw it, place the sheet on a couple of trestles, and cut it using a cross-cut hand saw. As the saw begins to bind in the cut, reach across the back of the saw and press the corner of the waste downwards with your left hand to ease the saw.

Mark off and plane the edges of the rectangular tray base, planing inwards from the corners. Check your work with a straightedge to make sure that the edges are straight.

■ Ends and Sides

Cut out cardboard templates for the end and side. Clamp both side blanks together, and drive two panel pins through the handholes to ensure an accurate location. Mark round the template, and cut out the curve with a jigsaw, fitted with a very fine, metal cutting sawblade. Do not hurry the cut, or the tip of the saw will wander off course. Repeat for the other pair of sides. Still in pairs, clamp them in the vice, and smooth off the sawcut with a block plane and file. Now drill a 12 mm (½ in) pilot hole in the centre of each handhold. Clamp the sides together and cut out the handholds with a fine narrow-bladed jigsaw. Repeat for the other sides. Separate the pieces and shape the upper edge of the lip and the inside edge of the handhold with a half-round file. Finish with sandpaper.

1st cut	1st STAGE	2ND.	3RD.

Rough shape with chisel.   Trim with plane.   Finish with rasp and sandpaper.

■ Hinges

Position over the centre section, scribe round with a knife, and chop out with a chisel. Screw the hinges with brass countersunk screws, lining up the heads with the outer edge of the tray. Fit the other hinges in the same way, but mark and remove all the hinges before finishing the tray.

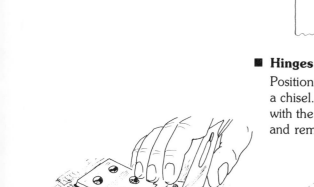
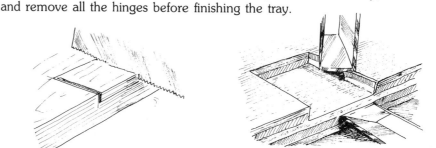

■ Finishing the Tray

Sand the plywood with 220 grit paper, finishing with 400 grit. Remove all file and sandpaper scratches.

■ Staining

Choose a suitably coloured mahogany stain which you should apply along the grain with a soft folded rag. Test the stain colour first on the underside of the tray or on an offcut of marine plywood. Some stains are too red, and you may have to add a little oak, or walnut stain to the mahogany to kill the red. Work round the edges once the main surface of the tray is stained, and finish with long even strokes up and down the flat surfaces. Leave the boards to dry, resting them on the points of drawing pins.

■ Sealing

Seal the wood with a shellac sealer. After leaving it to dry for 30 minutes, lightly rub down the surface with a scrap of 400 grit paper. Do not rub hard at the edges.

■ Filling

Fill the grain with coloured grain filler. This has to be pressed hard into the wood, to fill the small pores in the surface. If a commercial grain filler is not available, buy some plaster of paris from your local chemist and mix it with some brown powder paint. Pile the mixture in a saucer, dampen a rag with water and use the damp rag to pick up the plaster mix. Rub it onto the wood, working across the grain. Wipe away excess plaster with a clean rag, rubbing across the grain as before. The dry plaster will appear as white flecks in the surface of the dark mahogany. Very lightly rub over the surface with fine sandpaper, then rub a small quantity of linseed oil onto the tray; the plaster will turn transparent.

■ Varnishing

Apply varnish to one surface at a time. Rub down between coats, as recommended by the varnish manufacturers.

Fit the brasswork when you have finished varnishing. Leave the work for three or four days for the varnish to harden before polishing the surface with burnishing cream. Wax the tray with shoe polish.

■ Trestle

This is very easy to make. Choose straight-grained knot-free pine. Pre-drill the pivot holes before assembling. Stain with potassium permanganate dissolved in water. Staple or tack the upholstery webbing last.

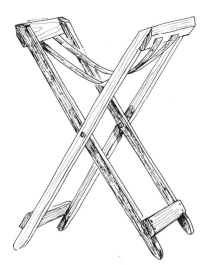

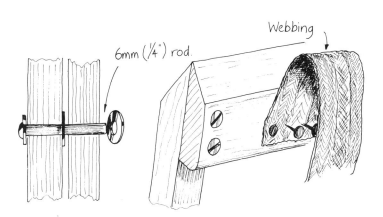

6mm (¼") rod.

Webbing

CLIMBING FRAME

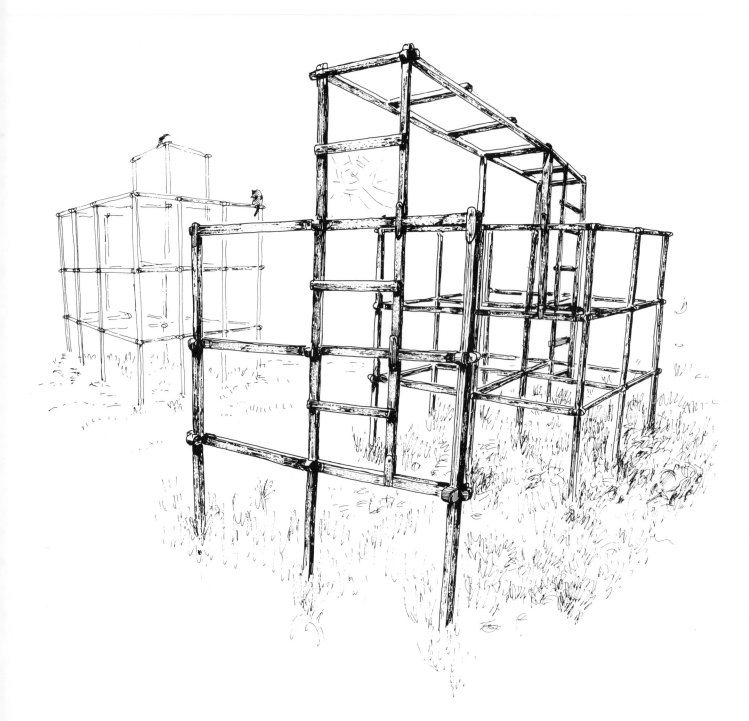

THERE are several suggested designs for a climbing frame illustrated below, all jointed together with the simple gusset plates that can be mass produced in the workshop with the router and a router box. They are permanent frames that are assembled on site, so although a lot of the preparatory work can be completed in the workshop, you must choose a fine hot day to assemble it.

CLIMBING FRAME

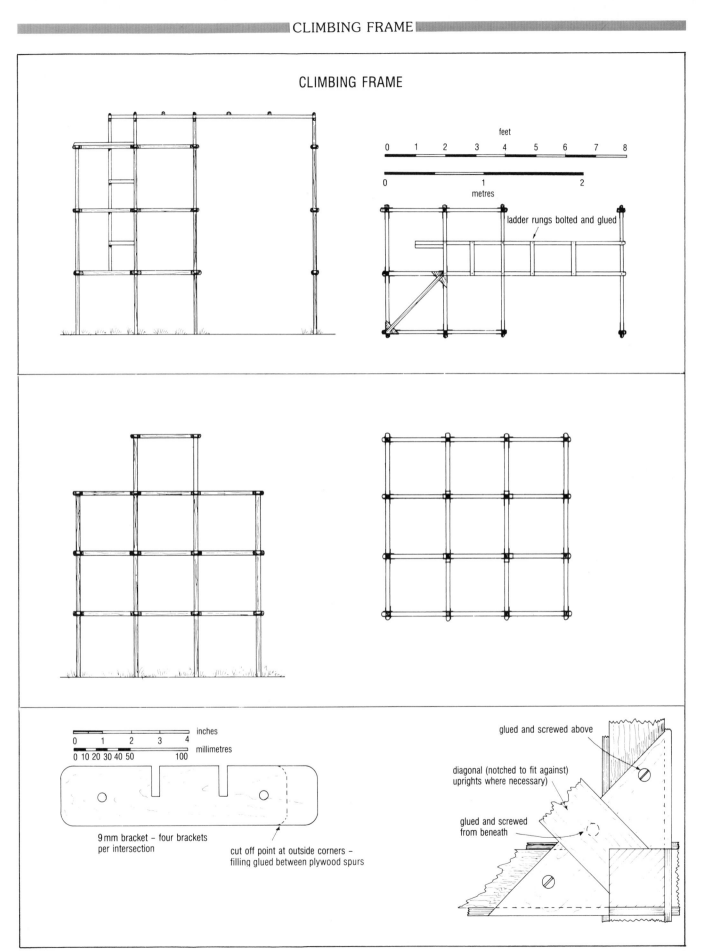

feet

0 1 2 3 4 5 6 7 8

0 1 2

metres

ladder rungs bolted and glued

9 mm bracket – four brackets
per intersection

cut off point at outside corners –
filling glued between plywood spurs

inches

0 1 2 3 4

0 10 20 30 40 50 100

millimetres

glued and screwed above

diagonal (notched to fit against)
uprights where necessary)

glued and screwed
from beneath

117

Use only the best materials. The wood should be straight-grained and knot-free. Douglas fir or sitka spruce is suitable; wood bought from a builder's merchant will have to be chosen extremely carefully. The wood must be strong, smooth and splinter-free.

The gussets are made from 9 mm (3⁄8 in) marine grade plywood. Ask your timber supplier to cut the strips to width and length.

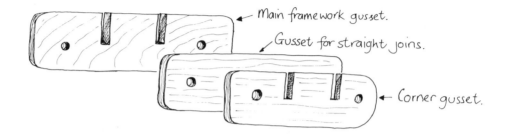

Main framework gusset.

Gusset for straight joins.

Corner gusset.

You will need to make two router boxes for shaping the gussets. The first one holds the gusset with retaining blocks around the outside, so that the slots can be routed out. The second box locates the gusset by the slots on one edge and with a block on its opposite edge, leaving the ends free for shaping.

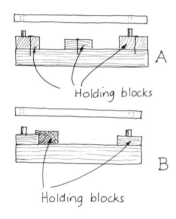

Holding blocks

A

Holding blocks

B

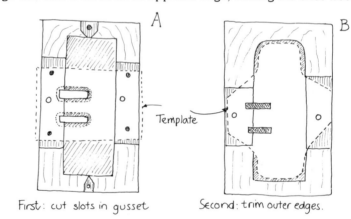

A

B

Template

First: cut slots in gusset

Second: trim outer edges.

Four interlocked gussets should clamp round a beam. The second gusset is equally easy to mass-produce, and only a few will be required.

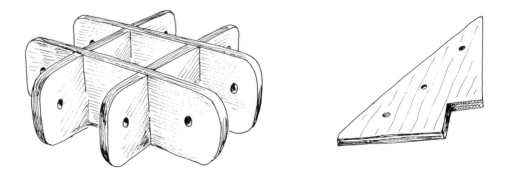

Once the design of the frame has been decided upon, calculate the number of gussets required. Cut the main beams to length and mark the location of each gusset. Champher and then sand the beams between joints.

Lay out the position for each leg, and dig a 450 mm (18 in) hole for each one. Sink a length of plastic drainpipe into each hole, with the top of each pipe just below the surface of the soil. If you drill a few holes in the sides of the pipe, you will be able to poke nails into the soil to improve its anchorage.

Apply a preliminary coat of epoxy resin over each component of the climbing frame, ensuring that end grain is well saturated. Choose a hot day for assembling the framework. You will need a supply of thixotropic epoxy resin, and a polyurethane foam dispenser, available from a D.I.Y. store or builder's mechant. Assemble the bottom rails and uprights, bolting, screwing or nailing the gussets, with the legs resting in the bottom of the plastic tubes. If the heights are incorrect, adjust them by dropping gravel down the tubes. As the structure grows, and the initial problems of setting out and erecting have been overcome, spray water into the tube and squirt some polyurethane foam

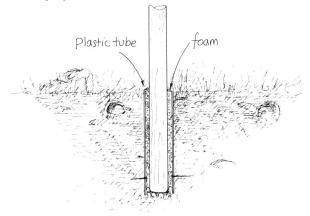

Plastic tube   foam

around each leg. This will bond the wood and the plastic tube together and form an almost impermeable barrier round the legs. Cut off the excess foam with a sharp knife, and paint the foam with a thick coat of exterior paint. Continue to assemble the climbing frame. Rest the diagonals on the right-angle gussets, which should be screwed to the horizontal beams as illustrated. Use plenty of glue, filletting the glue that has squeezed out with a shaped scraper. Fill the empty gussets with offcuts, rounding and sanding the ends. When the glue is cured, sand the entire framework and joints to remove splinters, etc. Then brush on two more coats of epoxy resin, applying the second coat as soon as the first is touch dry. Epoxy resin reaches full strength after about five days. Test the climbing frame before allowing children to clamber over it.

Excess glue filletted at edges.

FINISHING AND MAINTENANCE SCHEDULES

	MICROPOROUS PAINT FINISH
EXPLANATION	Microporous paints are designed for use out of doors. Even wood painted with a conventional paint finish absorbs and loses moisture when left outside. This movement of moisture, and the associated swelling and shrinking of the wood, quickly cracks and loosens a brittle non-porous finish. Microporous paints can flex, and allow moisture through without damage to the finish, while providing protection against excessive moisture absorption, and U.V. degradation of the wood.
WORK SEQUENCE	Fill all crevices with weatherproof filler, sand the furniture thoroughly and remove all dirt, dust and grease afterwards. Ensure that the furniture is dry.
PROTECTION	Brush on a copious coat of clear preservative. Soak the base of the legs in tubs of preservative for at least 3 minutes each leg. Apply a second coat after 2 hours and commence with finish after waiting 24 hours for the preservative to dry.
PRODUCT GUIDE SEALING	Ranch Preservative Clear (GDA 685). Apply weatherproof knotting to knots, resinous end grain, and cracks. Cedar and larch, in particular, exude an oily resin. It is worthwhile leaving furniture made from these woods in the sun for a few weeks, and then wipe off the resin with petrol or white spirit. Leave to dry and apply knotting.
FINISH PRODUCT GUIDE	International Ranch Paint. 10 Colours including black and white Thinners: white spirit. Drying time: 6 hours at room temperature. Over-coating: 16 hours. Microporous, sheen finish, effective up to three coats, then loses microporosity.
APPLICATION	Use well-loaded brush, apply thickly. One coat is sufficient, two looks better. Light sanding between coats.
MAINTENANCE	Finish should last about five years. Then lightly sand, wash off dust and leave to dry. Refinish with single coat.

The finishing and maintenance schedules outlined here should provide long term protection with a minimum of maintenance for the furniture you have made. Wood decays when it is exposed to air and water. The furniture featured in this book is designed to allow ventilation around and between the components, and to eliminate areas where moisture and debris collect. If the furniture is finished according to one of the schedules outlined here, it will last, despite having been made from non-durable woods.

MICROPOROUS STAIN FINISH	EPOXY SEAL
Microporous stains have the same qualities as the paints, but are translucent. Available in a range of colours which enhance the natural colour of the woods being used, while protecting the wood against ultra-violet degradation of its surface fibres (noticeable beneath a conventional varnish finish as a grey or brown discoloration of the wood surface, which is a prelude to the varnish cracking and flaking). This is a thick, easy to apply finish, which provides excellent protection.	A sealed epoxy finish encases the wood, and restricts the passage of moisture vapour into the wood to such an extent that any change within the wood itself is minimal. The epoxy resin penetrates into the wood fibres, and adheres there with the unequalled strength of one of the toughest and most durable wood bonding glues known. Epoxy resin is a clear amber. The third coat can be polished to a high gloss, but for maximum protection against UV radiation, an additional two coats of polyurethane varnish are recommended.
As for paint.	As for paint and ensure that the furniture is at about 12% moisture content.
As for paint.	Not required.
As for paint.	Not required unless the wood is particularly resinous, and then you should wash off the excess resin with West System Cleaning Solvent, and leave the wood to dry.
International Ranch Stain. Six wood colour stains. Thinners: white spirit. Drying time: 5 hours at room temperature. Overcoating time: 16–24 hours. Microporous sheen finish. Semi-transparent, up to four coats.	West Epoxy 105 with fast hardener 205. Colour: amber. Mix: mix five parts by weight of resin: one part by weight of hardener. Pot life mixed: 10–20 minutes depending on temperature and quantity mixed. Cure time: 5 hours at 212°C (70°F). Clean tools with West System Cleaning Solvent.
Apply by brush, rag or pad. Stain is thick and easy to apply and shade. This allows fading and matching of tones for colour uniformity.	Three coats required. Mix small quantity, apply quickly. Every part must be sealed. Rub down first coat with 220–240 grit paper. Re-coat, and apply third when second is touch dry. Sand lightly. Varnish with West System 100 UV inhibiting varnish. Two part polyurethane varnish. Mix: two parts resin, one part hardener (volume). Pot life: 5 hours. Two coats.
As for paint.	None required, provided integrity of finish is intact.

CUTTING LIST

WOOD SIZES (for use with the plans)

Letter	metric	imperial	Letter	metric	imperial
A	50 × 50 mm	2 × 2 in	I	16 × 75 mm	¾ × 3 in
B	22 × 100 mm	1 × 4 in	J	38 × 50 mm	1½ × 2 in
C	22 × 75 mm	1 × 3 in	K	47 × 100 mm	1¾ × 4 in
D	22 × 50 mm	1 × 2 in	L	25 × 25 mm	1 × 1 in
E	50 × 75 mm	2 × 3 in	M	12 mm	½ in exterior ply
F	50 × 100 mm	2 × 3¾ in	N	4 mm	3/16 in exterior ply
G	75 × 75 mm	3 × 3 in	O	25 × 18 mm	1 × ¾ in knot-free cedar or pine
H	22 × 150 mm	1 × 6 in			

NB: These are trade equivalents of stock sizes.

Project 1 GARDEN SEAT

	1.8 m (6 ft)	2.4 m (8 ft)	3 m (10 ft)
G	1		1
B	3	1	1
F	1		
H	1		
I	1	3	
C			3
E			1

Project 2 ORCHARD BENCH

	1.8 m (6 ft)	2.4 m (8 ft)	3 m (10 ft)
G	2	1	2
J	1	1	
K	1		3
I	2	4	
C		4	
B	1	1	

Project 3 GARDEN CHAIR

	1.8 m (6 ft)	2.4 m (8 ft)	3 m (10 ft)
A			1
B	1		
J	1		
E	1		
C	1		1

Project 4 ARMCHAIR

	1.8 m (6 ft)	2.4 m (8 ft)	3 m (10 ft)
E		1	
A	1		
B		1	
K	1		
F	1		
H	1		
I	1		1

Project 5 CONVERSATION CHAIR

	1.8 m (6 ft)	2.4 m (8 ft)	3 m (10 ft)
C	2*	2*	
B	2	2	
E			1
J	1		
D	1		
I	1	1	1
C		1	

* Knot-free for laminate

Project 6 FOLDING SEATS

Steamer: knot-free cedar, oregon pine, or hardwood
1 length: 3.8 m (12 ft) × 35 mm (1¼ in) × 400 mm (1 ft 3 in)

Planter: 3.8 m (12 ft) × 35 mm (1¼ in) × 400 mm (1 ft 3 in)

FOLDING BENCH

	1.8 m (6 ft)	2.4 m (8 ft)	3 m (10 ft)
E		4	1
C	1	3	

Project 7 LONG GARDEN TABLE

	1.8 m (6 ft)	2.4 m (8 ft)	3 m (10 ft)
G			1
B			1
E		3	
D	1		
C		4	1

Project 8 DOUGLAS TABLE

	1.8 m (6 ft)	2.4 m (8 ft)	3 m (10 ft)
B			2
C	1		1
A	1		

Project 9 BROOK HOUSE TABLE

	1.8 m (6 ft)	2.4 m (8 ft)	3 m (10 ft)
F	1	1	1
C		5	1
G			1
E	1		1
D		2	

Project 10 MONK'S SEAT
Round top

	1.8 m (6 ft)	2.4 m (8 ft)	3 m (10 ft)
F	3		
E	2		1
C	2		2
B	1		

Square top

	1.8 m (6 ft)	2.4 m (8 ft)	3 m (10 ft)
E		2	2
C		3	2
B			3

Project 11 TREE SEAT

Quantities for the seat, back and capping pieces will have to be added according to the diameter of tree and seat.

Vertical supports only

	1.8 m (6 ft)	2.4 m (8 ft)	3 m (10 ft)
A			3
D		1	2

Project 12 SUN LOUNGER

	1.8 m (6 ft)	2.4 m (8 ft)	3 m (10 ft)
B		2	
L	1	3	
D	1	3	3
F		1	

Project 13 PLANTER
Round top

	1.8 m (6 ft)	2.4 m (8 ft)	3 m (10 ft)
G			1
H			2
D	2		

Trellis

C		1	
O	8		3

Plus 12 mm (½ in) and 4 mm (³⁄₁₆ in) offcuts of exterior or marine ply.

Pointed

	1.8 m (6 ft)	2.4 m (8 ft)	3 m (10 ft)
G			1
H	1	1	
B	1		
D	1		

Box

	1.8 m (6 ft)	2.4 m (8 ft)
25 × 12 mm (1 × ½ in)	1	2

Plus 1 large sheet of exterior plywood 4 mm (³⁄₁₆ in) or 6 mm (¼ in).

Project 14 CRICKET TABLE

	1.8 m (6 ft)	2.4 m (8 ft)	3 m (10 ft)
B	1		
E		1	
I	1		
D	1		
K	1		

Note – top not included.

Project 15 BUTLER'S TRAY

Marine plywood 12 mm (½ in) and knot-free pine battens.

Project 16 CLIMBING FRAME

Marine plywood 9 mm (³⁄₈ in) and knot-free oregon pine, or suitable durable hardwood. Quantities vary according to design.

GLOSSARY

Bench hook
A wooden board which lodges against the edge of the bench to steady wood being sawn or chiselled.

Batten
A narrow, straight strip of wood.

Burnishing cream
A fine abrasive cream used for polishing.

Butt joint
Two boards glued edge to edge.

Champher
A narrow, decorative bevel worked on the corner of a leg or rail.

Covering board
An edging plank used to protect underlying structure.

Crest rail
Top rail of a chair, often curved and shaped.

Cure
To harden and achieve maximum strength (*see* glueing).

Dumbstick
Rectangular card or block used to transfer irregular shapes from one piece of wood to another.

Earpiece
Decorative strengthening piece glued at the joint of the leg and rail.

Epoxy resin
A versatile, weatherproof adhesive. Immensely strong.

Face
Trued side of a piece of wood.

Fence
Adjustable control to give a fixed distance for machining or marking wood.

Fielded panel
A panel with a raised centre and bevelled perimeter.

Finial
Decorative top to a leg or pillar.

Fluting
Vertical decorative stripes carved on a leg or pillar.

Following wheel
A routing attachment which keeps the router bit at a constant distance to the work. Used particularly where the workpiece is curved.

Groove
A channel carved or routed in the wood.

Gusset
A brace or support to strengthen an angle of framework.

Headstock
The pillar at one end of the lathe which holds the rotating head and motor.

Hone
To bring to a keen edge.

Jig
A roughly-constructed apparatus to enable work to be held to a machine, or to facilitate assembly.

Laminate
To build up by glueing strips of wood together.

Lip moulding
A round topped shallow edge.

Microporous finish
A coating which protects the wood from water, but allows moisture to escape from the wood.

Mitre
A joint between two pieces meeting, usually, at 90°. Each of the two pieces is cut to half the total angle.

Modular
Built from prefabricated units.

Offset
To set to one side by a fixed distance.

Peg
Tapered wooden dowel, used to pull and hold a joint together.

Pilot hole
A hole drilled into a piece of wood before screwing or nailing.

Potassium permanganate
A chemical stain, soluble in water. Turns mahogany a deep brown. Fugitive.

Punch
A tapered steel rod used for hammering a nailhead below the wood surface.

Rack and pawl
A device which permits adjustment by means of a hinged tooth and a series of notches.

Rail
Horizontal framework member.

Rasp
Rough toothed, sharp wood file.

Rebate
A recess along the edge of a piece of wood.

Resorcinol glue
A weatherproof exterior wood glue.

Router box
An open ended box, narrower than the router face plate, inside which workpieces can be clamped for routing. The router is steadied by the sides of the router box.

Routing board
A flat board with one raised straight edge, onto which small workpieces which have to be routed can be clamped prior to routing.

Saw cheeks
A pair of wooden boards used to hold a saw blade that is being sharpened.

Saw set
The degree by which saw teeth are bent to give the saw clearance.

Scarf
A long, sloping joint used to join boards end to end.

Shank hole
A hole the diameter of the upper unthreaded part of a screw shank, into which the screw will slip easily.

Shooting board
A carefully constructed board which assists accurate edge and end planing. One side is true, and there is a stop at right angles to that side against which the workpiece is pressed.

Shoulder
The end-grain edge of a joint.

Stretchers
Lengths of wood (often used as a foot rest) which connect and brace the legs of a table or chair.

Tailstock
Pillar at one end of the lathe, which incorporates the fixed point against which the revolving workpiece pivots.

Template
A pattern used for guiding a tool in repetitive work.

Thixotropic epoxy glue
A thick, easily-worked gap-filling glue, which does not run.

Thumbnail moulding
A small convex radius worked on the edge of a rail or table top.

SUPPLIERS

The following are available in the U.K.

Wood

Planed softwood in the exact sizes and lengths specified in these instructions is obtainable from your local Texas Homecare DIY Superstore.

Oak, cedar, sequoia, yew etc. from:
Interesting Timbers, Church Farm, Easton Grey, Malmesbury, Wiltshire, SN16 0PS.

Weatherproof glues

Wessex Resins and Adhesives, Wessex House, 189–193 Spring Road, Sholing, Southampton, Hampshire, SO2 7NY.

Exterior paints and stains

International Paints Ltd, 24–30 Canute Road, Southampton, Hampshire, SO9 3AS.

Wheels

Geo. H. Hughes Ltd, Edgemond Avenue, Birmingham, B24 0QX.

Brassware

John Lawrence and Co. (Dover) Ltd, Granville Street, Dover, Kent, CT16 2LF.

Tools

The tools needed to make the furniture described in this book are readily available in most ironmongers and DIY stores. For information on the full range of Bosch power tools, and their use, contact:

Robert Bosch Ltd, P.O. Box 98, Broadwater Park, North Orbital Road, Denham, Uxbridge, Middlesex, UB9 5HJ.

The following are available in the U.S.A.

Wood

Soft and hardwood
Maurice L. Condon Co. Inc., 248 Ferris Avenue, White Plains, NY 10603.

Glues

Resorcinol resin glue
Harbor Sales Co., 1401 Russell Street, Baltimore, Maryland 21230.

Urea-formaldehyde glue
Woodcraft Supply Corp., 313 Montvale Ave., Woburn, Mass. 01801.

West Epoxy System
Gougeon Brothers Inc., 706 Martin Street, Bay City, Michigan 48706.

Tools and Brassware

Woodcraft, 41 Atlantic Avenue, P.O. Box 4000, Woburn, Mass. 01888.

INDEX